D0467838

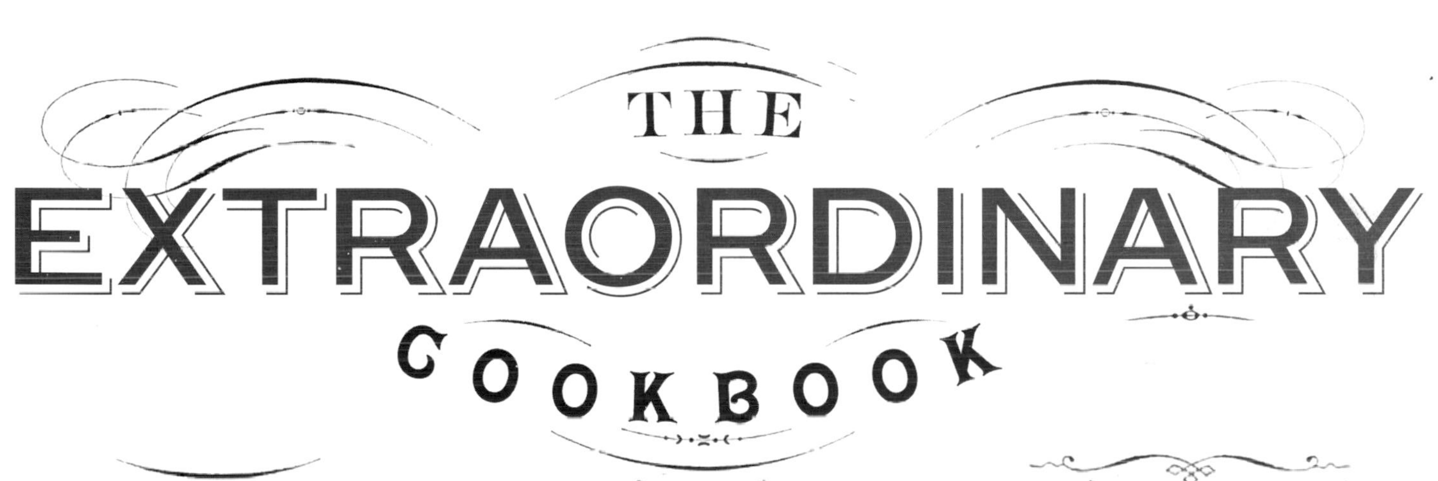
THE
EXTRAORDINARY
COOKBOOK

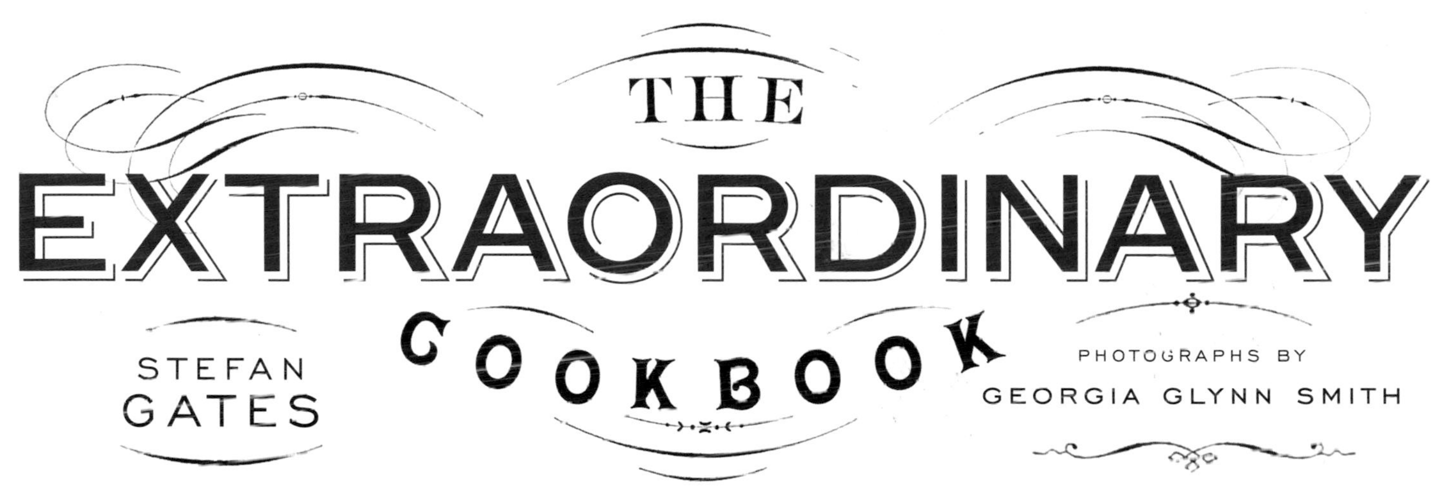

*HOW TO MAKE
MEALS YOUR
FRIENDS
WILL
NEVER
FORGET*

KYLE BOOKS

To Poppy, Daisy, and Georgia
For making it all so much fun

To you
For joining in

Published in 2011 by Kyle Books
www.kylebooks.com

Distributed by National Book Network
4501 Forbes Blvd., Suite 200
Lanham, MD 20706
Phone: (800) 462-6420; Fax: (301) 429-5746
custserv@nbnbooks.com

First published in Great Britain in 2010 by Kyle Books
ISBN 978-1-906868-40-6

Project editor: Jenny Wheatley
Photographer: Georgia Glynn Smith
Designer: Two Associates
Food stylist: Marina Filippelli
Props stylist: Lyndsay Milne Mcleod
Americanizer: Margaret Parrish
Copy editor: Anne McDowall
Editorial assistant: Elanor Clarke
Production: Gemma John

Library of Congress Control Number: 2011926468

Printed in China by C & C Offset Printing Co.

CONTENTS

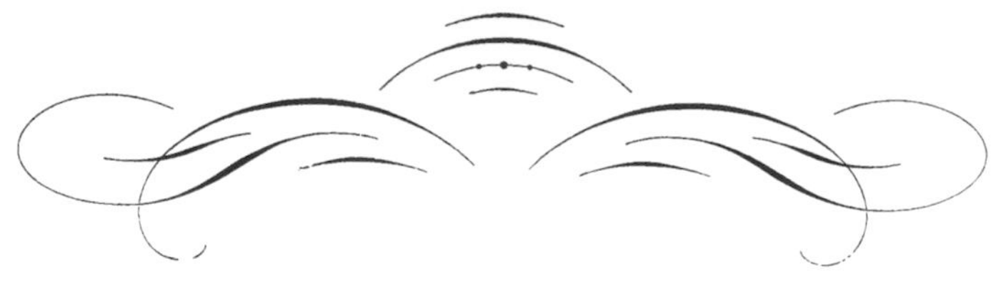

HELLO

I have two humble ambitions in writing this book:

1. To blow your mind.
2. To transform your meals into adventures.

Despite what you might think, it's actually pretty easy to create meals that your friends will never forget. You don't need to spend lots of time or money, but you do need some inspiration and a little handholding, and that's what this book is for. All the recipes here are practical and thoroughly achievable—nothing is included simply as a flight of fancy or to make the book look impressive, and, although you might save a few of these dishes for a special occasion, the vast majority are meals that I make on a daily basis at home. Hang on—there is the obvious exception of liquid nitrogen ice cream, which, it's true, is an indulgent frill. But that's about it.

There are a few dishes that sound challenging, such as Apple Caviar, Crispy Jellyfish and Beansprout Salad, and Skewers Cooked on a Car Engine, but I urge you not to underestimate your family and friends' tolerance for adventures, and your ability to create them. You'll be surprised how even the pickiest eaters (especially kids) jump at the chance of an exhilarating culinary escapade, and that, despite appearances, even dishes such as Golden Chicken can be easy and relatively cheap to make.

Often, the key to unlocking the exhilaration in food is to rethink the way it's cooked and served. Can you get your friends to take part in the process? Can they interact with their food, perhaps in a way that they haven't before, by churning their own butter in a jam jar, by rolling their own sushi, by creating their own soup, or by trying an ingredient like jellyfish that they'd never normally eat? Because that's the key to giving your friends an enlightening and unforgettable experience: by flattering their intelligence and feeding their appetite for adventure.

My favorite meals in this book are probably the ones in which my friends get thoroughly (often messily) involved. Every single time I've thrown a sushi rolling night, shabu-shabu feast, or hammer-and-crab riot, the evening has transformed from a dinner into a party. When people really get a handle on their food, they have a sensual as well as social experience, and they lose their inhibitions. And that, my friends, is all you need; the rest of your adventure will follow as a matter of course.

Sharing food is vital to my happiness and I'm sure it is to yours as well. Whether you make Chicken Liver Parfait, Vegetable Instruments, or Fluorescent Jello, or you serve a simple bowl of peas still in their pods or the world's finest bellota jamón Iberico, I truly believe that unforgettable and extraordinary meals shared with the people you love are some of the most wonderful experiences life has to offer.

I've had a fantastic time writing this book. I hope you enjoy it and that it leads you to some extraordinary experiences. If it does, I want to know all about them. Drop me a line at www.thegastronaut.com.

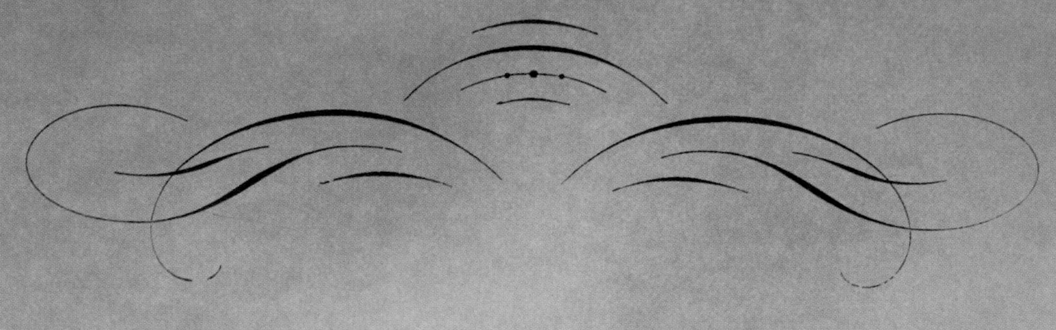

1

SNACKS

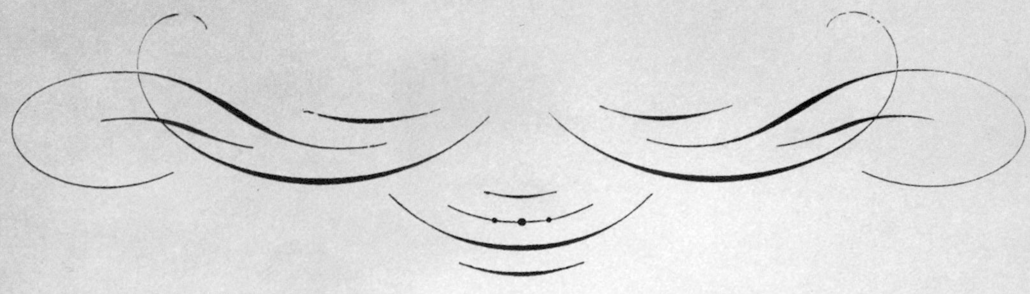

I LIKE DINNERS AT MY HOUSE TO BE relaxed but exhilarating affairs, so when you come over for supper you'll inevitably arrive to merry chaos, with the kids up way too late (refusing to go to bed until they've met you), loud music on the stereo, my head in the oven (in a good way), and little samples of food all over the place because I wanted you to try something new that I've found. Likely as not, you'll be roped in to read the kids a story, toast some chestnuts, carve a butternut bassoon, or whittle a radish mouse. This might sound a bit slack, but there's a good reason for it: I want you to feel involved and relaxed and I don't want you to spend a single moment worrying what you're going to say or who you're going to sit next to. I do have two unbreakable rules, for myself to follow: the table must be set (I want you to feel welcome and expected), and there should always be some snacks to nibble on. Little nuggets of magical tastes and little bombs of flavor or possibly something extraordinary or adventurous to tickle your taste buds. These are foods to eat with your hands, to get you licking your fingers, and to warm you up for the adventures to come. I want you to drop your defenses, to prime yourself for adventure, and to get ready for a meal that you'll never forget.

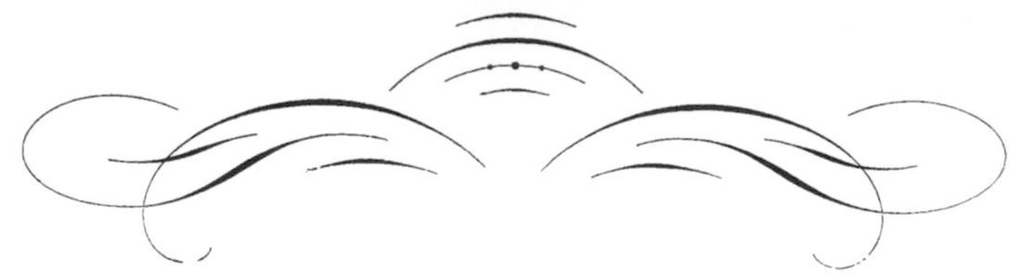

BLOODY MARY TOMATOES

Be very careful when you pass these around, since they are disarmingly tasty and sneakily alcoholic. They are also perfectly bite-sized, so you'll find yourself popping them into your mouth one after the other like grapes, and, before you know it, you and your friends will be completely legless.

The following story is a salutary lesson—and too funny to keep to myself. A few years ago, we held a big lunch party after my daughter's baptism, and the lovely vicar kindly agreed to come along, accompanied by the equally lovely lady minister. Anyone who thought their presence might add a little gravity to the situation was to be sorely disappointed, however. It all started when the Bloody Mary tomatoes came out, and both vicar and minister tucked in with great enthusiasm. It's *possible* that I forgot to mention that the tomatoes were packed with vodka, but anyone could have been forgiven for thinking that they were just very tasty. And, of course, vodka can be strangely hard to detect, especially when you've got a glass of wine in the other hand.

Anyway, both vicar and minister enjoyed the tomatoes enormously, so much so that by the time they sat down to eat they were already slurring their words. The vicar struck up a ferocious theological argument with the minister and before long I heard him use a phrase that was, well, let's just say, it was very naughty. Upon hearing himself utter said phrase, it dawned on him that perhaps it was time to leave. He and the minister thanked us all profusely and ambled out. A few moments later, we heard an enormous crash, and we all raced out to the hallway to find the vicar and the minister rolling on the floor in fits of giggles, having knocked a large picture off the wall. Luckily, damage was done to neither property nor preacher, so I gave them both a hug and sent them wandering off down the street.

SERVES 6

- 30 ripe cherry tomatoes (about 2lb), the tastiest you can find
- 1 ½ cups good vodka
- ¼ cup sherry (optional—if you don't have any, replace with vodka)
- 1 tablespoon Worcestershire sauce
- 1 teaspoon Tabasco sauce
- 1 teaspoon freshly grated horseradish (optional)
- 4 fresh thyme sprigs (optional)
- celery salt and table salt, to serve

Prick each tomato several times using a toothpick. In a bowl, mix together the vodka, sherry, Worcestershire sauce, Tabasco sauce, horseradish, and thyme.

Place the tomatoes in a large jar (or several small jars), then pour over the marinade until they are covered. (If necessary, add a little more vodka so that all are submerged.) Leave for at least two days. The tomatoes get a little wizened and overly alcoholic after a few weeks, and by the time they are a month old, they are over the hill and should be put in a food processor with chopped tomatoes to make a ferocious Bloody Mary.

Serve the tomatoes with a small dipping bowl of equal measures of celery salt mixed with table salt.

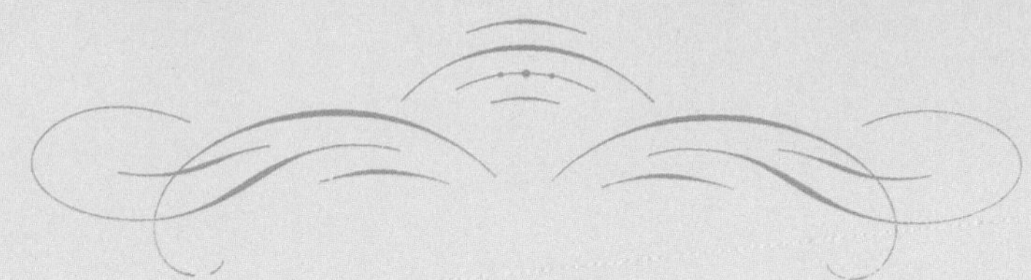

BOWLS OF PEA PODS OR EDAMAME BEANS

It's not exactly a recipe, is it? But when you place a bowl of pea pods on the table for your friends to tuck into, something small but revelatory happens. Your friends start their meal by touching something organic rather than metallic—food rather than fork—and they immediately interact with it (if that's not too grand a word for "playing with your food"). Of course, you could just get your guests to do some work for you by shelling peas to accompany the main course. (I always like to hand out a few tasks like this, since it's a way to get people chatting at the start of an evening.)

EDAMAME BEANS

Unlike pea pods, edamame (pronounced "ed–a-mahmay") are best cooked before serving. They are green soybeans, and you can buy them frozen from Japanese and Chinese stores in 2lb bags.

If you've bought frozen beans, check the package to see if they've been cooked before freezing; they usually have been. If they've been precooked, just throw them in a large pan of boiling water and as soon as the water comes back to a boil, drain. If they have been frozen raw, or if you have bought fresh beans, throw them into a large pan of boiling water, bring the water back to a boil, and simmer the beans for 3–4 minutes before draining. Sprinkle the cooked beans with salt and soy sauce before serving.

RUSSIAN ROULETTE PADRÓN PEPPERS

These beautiful little peppers, about the size of a thumb, are fantastic to serve as a snack alongside a glass of chilled manzanilla or oloroso sherry. However, it's not just their taste that makes them extraordinary, but also the fact that around one in 12 of them is hot enough to give you an exciting jolt of capsaicin (the active ingredient in chiles).

They are traditionally grown around the village of Padrón in Galicia, northwestern Spain, although you can now find them all over the world, and the seeds are widely available, so you can even grow them in your garden (see Suppliers, page 218). Debate rages over the proportion of hot peppers in each batch, some people claiming 1:10 and others 1:50. I've eaten them when every other one seems to have a big chile kick, but when I staged a game of Russian roulette peppers on a TV show, not a single one turned out to be hot, much to my annoyance. It didn't really matter, though, because they were so sweet and complex in flavor that their deliciousness made up for it.

SERVES 6

1lb bag of Padrón peppers (often sold as *pimientos de Padrón*)
3 tablespoons olive oil
salt (preferably flaky sea salt)

Heat the olive oil in a large frying pan, then fry the peppers a large handful at a time, until the skins start to blister and brown. Be careful though, since they can spit and pop in the oil. Remove, rest on a paper towel to remove any excess oil, scatter liberally with sea salt, and serve hot.

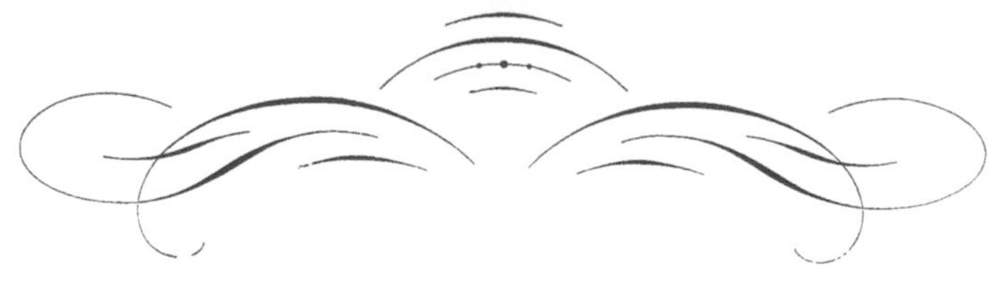

RADISH MICE

Considering the extraordinary design of the radish—with the contrast between its vivid fuchsia outer skin and pure white innards—it was only a matter of time before people started using it for art. The classic book on playing with food like this is the wonderfully kooky, slightly twisted, German *Du Mont's Phantasievoller Ratgeber für Vergnugte Koche* (Imaginative Guide for the Happy Cook).

Use superfresh radishes and keep them in the refrigerator until you serve them to keep them from becoming droopy. These mice are great as a little snack before dinner, but also as an accompaniment to a plate of cheese. It might sound a little silly, but if your friends are cool enough to play, it's fun to let people make their own mice.

Wash the radishes, but leave the stringy "tail" on and cut the greenery off to leave behind a stubby green nose and maybe a few whiskers. Cut a base off each radish (this will help it stay upright) and then cut two small disks from that base offcut for ears. Make two small cuts in the head end of the radish and stick the ears into them. Spike some eye-socket holes with the prong of a fork, then push two peppercorns in to form the eyes. Store the mice in the fridge until needed. Warning: Don't eat the peppercorns!

RADISHES AND ALMONDS WITH SALT

Radishes have a fantastic hot bite and are delicious scrubbed and eaten just as they are, dipped in salt. The same works for almonds, and if you ever manage to find young almonds still in their green shells (or can help yourself to a few from the tree), you will be in for a little slice of heaven. Crack open the shells (a strong set of teeth should do it, although careful of the dental work!) and pick out the creamy nut inside, then dip it in the tiniest amount of salt crystals.

SERVES 6

2 bunches of fresh radishes
2 handfuls of fresh almonds or walnuts
 (if in season, optional)
sea salt, for dipping

Pull the larger leaves off the radishes, leaving some stem behind. Wash and drain. Serve (with the almonds if you managed to find them) with a small bowl of salt for dipping.

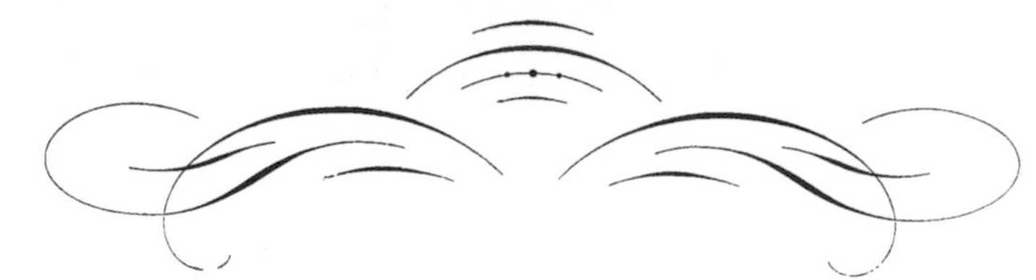

PICKLED EGG IN A BAG OF CHIPS

My friend Nick often serves this at The Drapers Arms, which just happens to be my favorite pub in London. There's something exhilaratingly childish about being given a pickled egg, a bag of chips, and the license to squish them together to make a gloriously heady, vinegary mess.

This does seem to be mainly (although not exclusively) a boy thing, and an early Eighties boy thing at that. Ignore the disapproving glances of wife/girlfriend (or husband/boyfriend, should you be bucking the trend) and open up a tangy bag of salt and vinegar chips. Drop the pickled egg inside and gently squish the bag so that the egg breaks up but doesn't disintegrate entirely. Then sit back, hold pint of beer in one hand, and tuck into the package without an ounce of shame.

PICKLING YOUR OWN EGGS

a large jar
eggs (as many as will fit into your jar)
4 bay leaves
6 garlic cloves, peeled
malt vinegar
1 teaspoon black peppercorns

Put the eggs into a saucepan of cold water, bring to a boil and simmer for about 7 minutes (but for no longer than 10 minutes, or the yolks will become gray). Transfer to a large pan of cold water to cool them and keep them from overcooking.

Crack the shells, peel the eggs, and add them to the jar with the bay leaves and garlic. Pour over enough malt vinegar to cover them and then sprinkle the peppercorns on top. Seal the jars and label them with the date. You can eat them within two days, although they are best left for two weeks and can be eaten for up to one year later.

ERVED
NEW
BROW

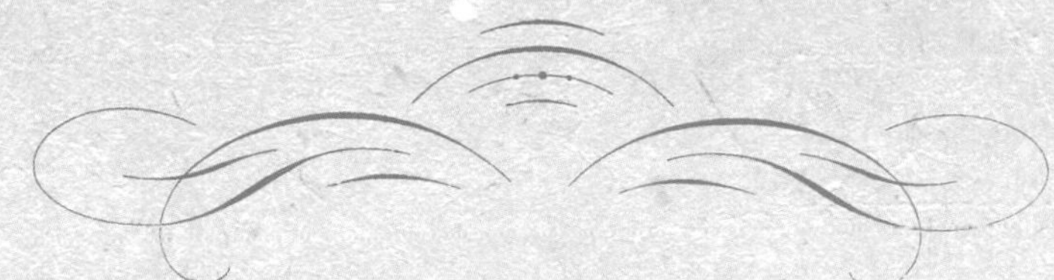

TOOTHPICK CANAPÉS FOR THE EXTRAORDINARY WORLD

The word "canapé" always reminds me of pineapple and cheese on a toothpick, jabbed into a foil-covered potato and served in a retro Seventies belief that it's the height of sophistication. I know I'm supposed to think that's tacky, but I'm a product of the Seventies, and I have to admit that I really like the fruit-cheese combination. So, here are a few ideas for updating the canapé and bringing it into the new millennium.

- Blue Stilton with ripe pear cubes (tossed in a little lemon juice to keep them from turning brown).
- Lancashire cheese with cubes of Christmas fruitcake (believe me, this is fantastic, like the classic combination of Lancashire cheese and the English pastry Eccles cake).
- Manchego with a little square of membrillo (quince cheese or paste).
- Cubes of Parmesan on their own, with a little bowl of balsamic vinegar for dipping.
- Sharp Cheddar cheese with apple cubes (tossed in a little lemon juice to stop them from turning brown). Go on, call me old-fashioned.

HOT TOASTED ALMONDS

It's a simple idea, but a plate of nuts that have been quickly roasted in the oven provides a hit of really good flavors, and combined with a glass of good sherry, it's a sparkling way to start an evening.

¾lb whole almonds, skins on
2 tablespoons olive oil
1 teaspoon sweet smoked paprika (optional)
1 teaspoon sea salt

Preheat the oven to 350°F. Put the almonds, olive oil, and paprika together in a bowl and mix around so the almonds are all nicely coated in oil and spice, then spread them out on a baking sheet.

Roast them in the oven for 20 minutes, stirring them every 5 minutes. Remove from the oven and place on paper towels to remove any excess oil, then sprinkle them with salt to taste. Serve with chilled manzanilla or oloroso sherry.

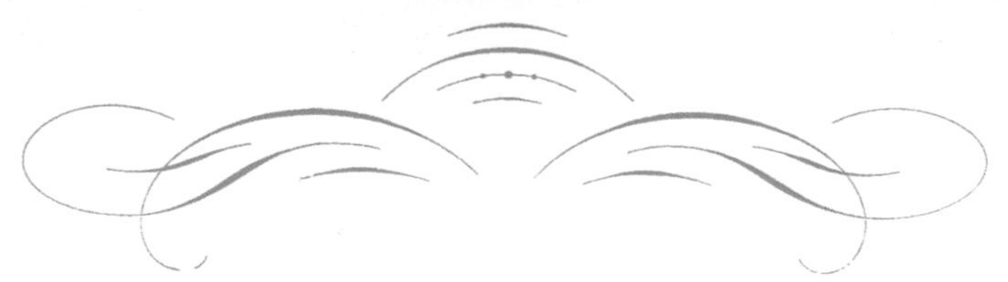

SEA VIOLETS AND SEA URCHINS

Sea urchins are pretty rare at the fish market's counter, and sea violets even rarer, but they are such an extraordinary and unlikely looking food that I thought you should know about them in case you ever stumble across them while foraging, or perhaps find yourself sitting in front of a *plateau de fruits de mer* at a sun-kissed island in the Mediterranean.

THE VIOLET is a type of sea squirt (Latin name: *microcosmus sabatieri*). The French call them violets or *figues de mer* (sea figs), in Spanish they are *patatas de mar* (sea potatoes), and in Italian *limone di mare* (sea lemons). Whatever you call them, they are bizarre little creatures. At my favorite seafood shop they squeeze then lightly so they squirt seawater over the kids, causing yelps of joy. You simply cut them open (watch out—they usually squirt at you somehow) to reveal a texture oddly similar to egg yolk, but with a sweet and almost ammonia-ey zing to them. Squeeze lemon juice over them and eat them raw, digging the innards out with a teaspoon.

SEA URCHINS (below left) are little spiny beasts that lurk in the water, waiting to spear your pinky toes when you're least expecting it. They are related to sea stars and sea cucumbers (they are members of the phylum *Echinodermata*, meaning spiny skin) and they move around the seabed on hundreds of tiny adhesive feet. If you find a live one, you can stroke the spines with a knife and watch them slowly ripple as a reaction. In France, they are known as *oursins*; in Maine, they are called whore's eggs.

Sea urchins must be cut open with a pair of scissors—a tricky and prickly job, for which a pair of gardening gloves comes in handy. They taste delicious, although only the larger ones yield a decent amount of food, and even they could only ever be described as a snack. The five little yellowey/orangey lobes inside are the ovaries, or corals, and these are the edible parts, usually eaten raw straight from the urchin. They are also fantastic mixed with scrambled eggs, and I've eaten them in Japan as sushi. The taste is extraordinary—as if seawater has been turned solid and sweet by a wave of Neptune's trident.

LAGUIOLE ORIGINE
GARANTIE
LAGUIOLE

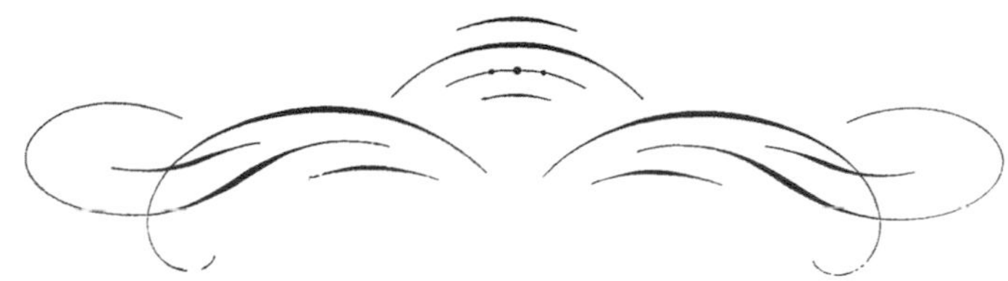

THAI-FLAVORED OYSTERS SERVED IN A SPOON

These are ridiculously good. You can, of course, serve them in the oyster shell if you like, but there's something fun about using these Asian flat-bottomed spoons as mini bowls.

A WORD ON OYSTER SHUCKING

Opening oysters really doesn't have to be painful and difficult. If you manage to buy oysters with relatively flat, regular lips (the lip is the wide end of the oyster as opposed to the pointed end), you should be able to slip a flat butter knife through the thin shell from the lip end with minimal damage to the oyster. Here's a remarkably effective method I learned from a friend in France (change indicated hands if you're left-handed):

Place a dish towel across your upturned left hand, then place the oyster on your covered palm, with the flatter side up and the pointed end facing away from you. Gripping the sides of the oyster, and with your hand resting on a sturdy surface, dig a flat butter knife into the top edge of the lip nearest you and through into the cavity of the oyster. You should be able to do this without causing much damage at all, as long as your oysters are relatively flat-lipped.

Gently wriggle the knife into the oyster, keeping the blade at the top of the interior, then slice across from right to left to cut the main muscle that keeps the oyster shut. You may have to do some digging around for the first one, until you get the hang of it.

Pry the top shell off, then spill the smallest splash of the oyster's juices out of the shell and across the cut that you made to the shell to wash away any stray bits of shell.

Gently cut under the oyster flesh to release it from the lower shell.

If your oysters are rough and gnarly looking you might have to resort to going in from the pointed end using a strong, pointed knife, but this generally causes more damage.

MAKES 12 SPOONS

1 scallion, finely sliced
1 lemongrass stem, outer leaves removed, very finely sliced
1 teaspoon Thai fish sauce (nam pla)
1 teaspoon toasted sesame oil
1 tablespoon vegetable oil
½ clove garlic, very finely chopped
½ chile, seeds removed and very finely chopped
zest and juice of 1 lime
zest and juice of ½ orange
a handful of cilantro, finely chopped
12 medium-sized rock oysters

Put all the ingredients except the oysters together in a bowl and stir to combine (or put in a jam jar and shake vigorously). Set aside to infuse for half an hour while you prepare your oysters.

Shuck the oysters as described at left, then remove the oysters from the shells and place one in each spoon or oyster shell. Sit the spoons on a tray that will fit in your refrigerator. Spoon over the infused sauce and store in the fridge until ready to serve.

Tip: If you're serving them in oyster shells, serve them on a bed of crushed ice or rock salt to keep them upright.

CHARCUTERIE

My kids love French *saucisson sec* with such a passion that I have to lock it away from them, since they'll inevitably wolf it all down if it's left unattended.

It's a great idea to invest in a small selection of good charcuterie to keep in stock, and just slice a few very thin slivers from each sausage as needed to lay on a wooden cutting board alongside some olives or toasted almonds. Charcuterie translates as "cooked meats" (which is slightly misleading, since most hams, *saucisson*, and salami are cured in salt then air-dried without ever being cooked using heat).

Charcuterie makes a great appetizer, especially when the flavors of the meal you're planning are good and robust (I wouldn't serve it before sushi, since the saltiness and intensity of the flavors will blow away the delicacy of the fish). Store your sausages in the fridge. There are some excellent varieties available, and you can get some wonderful combinations of pork with figs, nuts, wild boar, venison, and the like. My favorite is a French one called *figuetel*, which is made with extra pig's liver, which is extraordinarily intense.

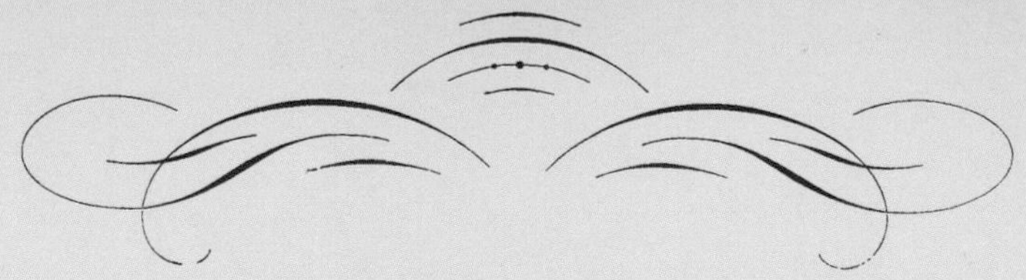

FOR THE LOVE OF JAMÓN

Whole legs and shoulders of air-cured ham make me go weak in the knees, and I usually have at least one in stock at home. You can buy basic, relatively inexpensive ones that are perfectly enjoyable or you can spend a king's ransom on a superb Joselito Gran Reserva Bellota acorn-fed Pata Negra and fly to gustatory heaven on a nightly basis. A cured ham is not that expensive when you consider that it will last several months and supply you with dozens of meals, and the flavor is so intense that you only need a few slices to feel as though you've eaten a feast. A whole leg of ham on the bone is a beautiful thing to behold, too. I'll often put the whole thing in front of a friend who arrives early for supper and set them to work cutting thin slivers of it. Choose one of your more dexterous friends and supply a long, firm ultrasharp knife. This ham is mind-blowingly good when nibbled with a glass of manzanilla sherry.

If you do invest in a whole leg of cured ham, you'll need to buy or make a sturdy little stand for it, otherwise it will be a pain to carve. I have a few stands that came free with the legs, and, although the kitchen-gadget lover in me does yearn for the Jamotec J4 (the dream machine of ham stands), you certainly don't have to splurge on an expensive one. The cheaper ones (see Suppliers, page 218) will last for years, and a sturdy make-your-own model might also suffice, as long as it has a grip to hold the hoof and a good spike for the meaty end to sit on.

STORING A WHOLE LEG OF HAM

If your ham arrives vacuum-sealed it will last unopened for about six months if kept in a cool place. Once opened, wipe any moisture and natural mold off and store it in a cool place, ideally at around 50–60°F. It should last for three months, although it gradually dries out. If you can, try to get a bone-in ham, rather than a boned one, as the latter will lose its structure after you've cut three-quarters of the meat off. If you have bought a boned ham, it's probably best kept in the fridge (if you have one that's big enough).

Once you've started cutting into the ham, save a few large, flat slices of fat to lay over the exposed meat, to slow down the drying-out process, and cover this with a dry dish towel.

A LITTLE SECRET...

While writing this piece, I got very excited about Pata Negra (Iberian blackfoot) ham, which is so expensive that I normally buy only a few slices several times a year as a special treat. A whole Pata Negra leg costs about the same as a decent second-hand car, but I've discovered that you can also buy shoulders, which are less costly, from the great Pata Negra producers (see Suppliers, page 218). They have less meat and a little more connective tissue, but they still have that all-important depth of flavor and long-lingering delightful aftertaste of the real thing. Even a shoulder isn't exactly what you'd call cheap, but there's still a little cash left over for the kids' shoes—if they leave any ham for me, that is. And here's another tip: I tend to get my little daughter to click the final "order" button on the website. That way I can blame her for laying out so much cash.

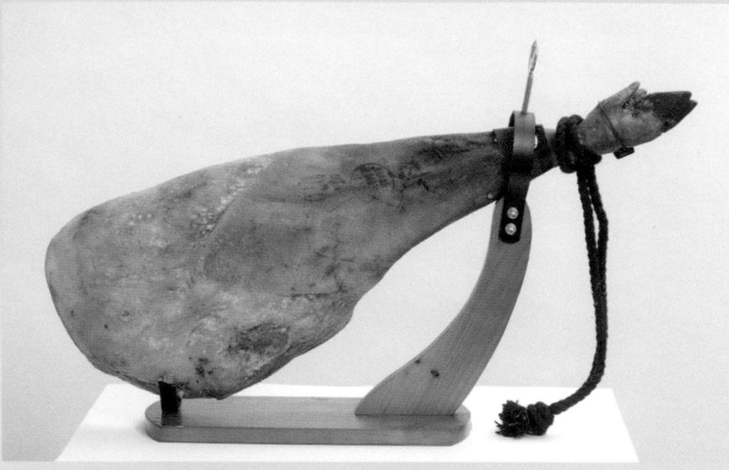

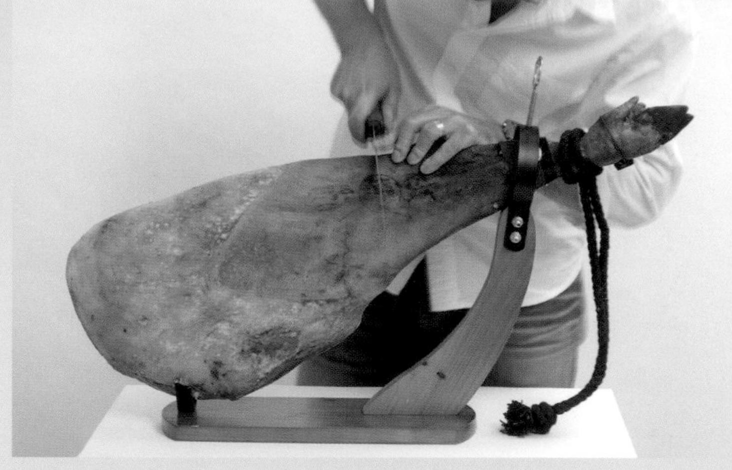

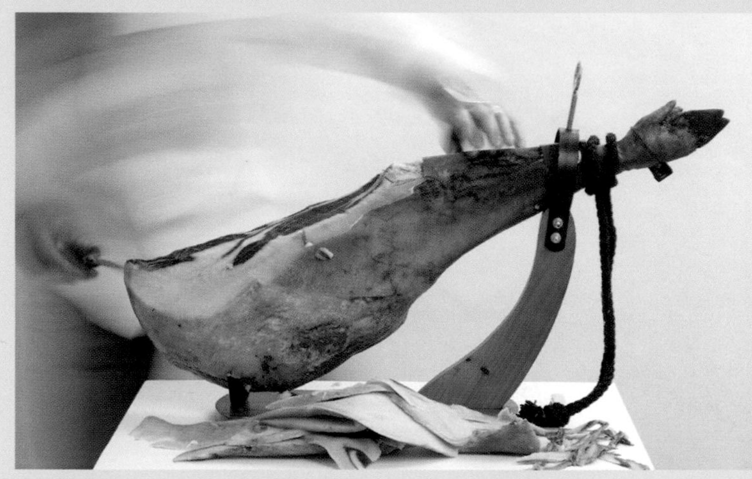

HOW TO CUT A WHOLE LEG OF HAM

I favor the Spanish method of cutting short thin slivers about 2in long, rather than trying to cut pieces the length of the ham. It's easier to eat, and it makes the whole process less stressful! Place the leg in a stand with the back of the hoof facing up (i.e., with the front of the calf facing downward).

Using a short, sharp knife, cut the skin and fat off around the top of the leg to reveal the meat inside (keep the fat for cooking). This is the tricky part, and there's a fair amount of pulling and hacking, since the skin is tough, but once you're in, it gets much easier.

Now, cut the fat from the top of the leg in a few large flat pieces, if you can, reserving it for protecting the exposed meat from drying out. When you get down to the meat, begin carving across in small pieces, whittling down until you start getting small slices about 2in long, cutting from the hoof end toward the thigh, and keeping the fatty edges on each piece (they are to be eaten, too). Try to keep the surface flat where you can. You'll need to cut around the pelvic bone or shoulder blade when you get to it, but don't try to cut these bones out—it's too destructive. Cut away more of the skin as you need to, and when you've cut every bit from one side, turn the leg over and start on the other side.

You can't eat much from around the hock end, but save it to make an extraordinary, intensely flavored ham and pea soup. Be warned, though: The ham has been heavily salted before drying, so don't add any salt to your soup until you're sure it's needed.

After each carving session, cover the exposed meat with fat or parchment paper and cover that with a dish towel and store somewhere cool.

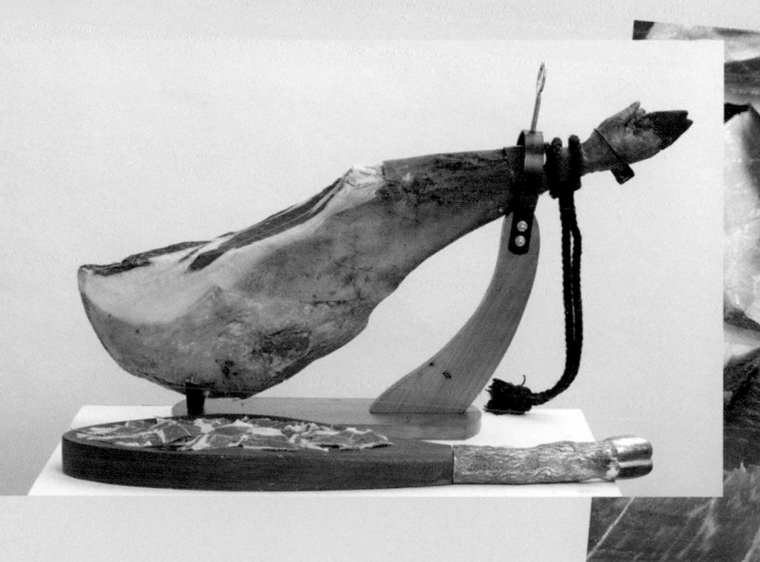

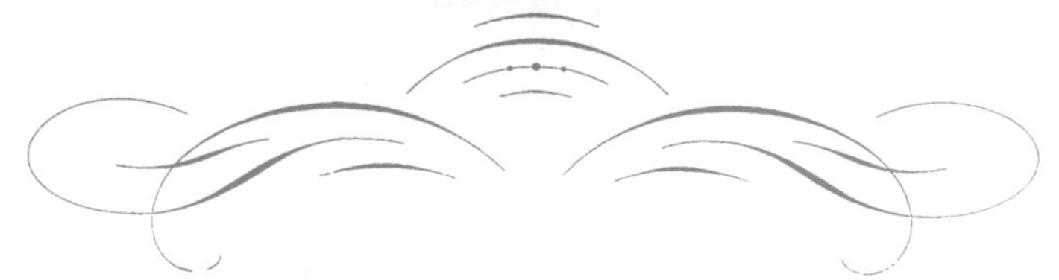

HOLEY-PAN-ROASTED CHESTNUTS

The smell of roasting chestnuts reminds me of Christmas far more than pine, chocolate, or spice. I remember eating these as a kid walking down London's Oxford Street in the falling snow, wrapped up in layers of wool against the bitter cold and desperately wishing that I could be taken to Hamleys toy store, but warmed by a charred handful of pungent chestnuts.

When you buy these on Oxford Street in London, they are usually roasted on a brazier, and their smell is their best advertisement. I always thought it would be impossible to get that smell at home, but when I met my wife, she showed me her rusty pans (an unconventional courting move, to be sure). They had holes drilled in them. I initially thought they were improvised colanders, but. of course, they were chestnut-roasting pans, and very beautiful they are, too.

THE HOLEY-PAN METHOD

Use this method for open fires, gas stoves, bonfires, and barbecues. Pick up an old uncoated metal pan from a secondhand store (or sacrifice an exhausted one of your own), and drill lots of holes in it, about the width of a pencil.

Cut little crosses into the chestnuts, either on the sides or at the base. This is to stop them from exploding, which is very likely to happen unless you give the steam a route to escape.

Place the chestnuts in a holey pan and place the pan over a fire. (This method also works happily over a normal gas stove.) Watch the pan throughout cooking, shaking it every now and then to prevent the chestnuts from burning too much—you want them to char but not burn to a cinder.

It will take around 10–20 minutes for them to cook, depending on the size of the nuts and the heat of the flame, during which time the nominated cook—not your good self, as you'll probably be elsewhere cooking something extraordinary—should be plied with glasses of port. Test one chestnut for tenderness and then leave the whole bunch to cool a little before serving with some salt.

OVEN METHOD

Preheat the oven to 400°F. Cut little crosses in the chestnuts as described before, then place them in a roasting pan and cook uncovered for 20–30 minutes.

Roasted chestnuts are best eaten still warm to the touch and peeled by the eater. We like dipping them in a little bowl of sea salt.

VEGETARIAN
ABALONE SLICES
鮑魚片
INSTANT
自然派
NATURAL IS BEST
KASUGAI
ROASTED
HOT GREEN PEAS
NET WT. 3.06 oz.
(87g)
新鮮パック
豆菓子
桜えび
お好み焼き、焼きそば、かき揚げに
内容量
13g
無着色
ORIENTAL FORTUNE
Bun Mini
Lotus
8
Tanpa Pengawet
海蜇頭
DELICIOUS JELLY FISH HEAD
美味
新鮮
YEO'S
Jelly Drink
清涼爽
Crispy
White Sardines
Lamthong
RAMBUTAN
STUFF WITH PINEAPPLE
CRISPY
BABY CLAM
& ANCHOVY

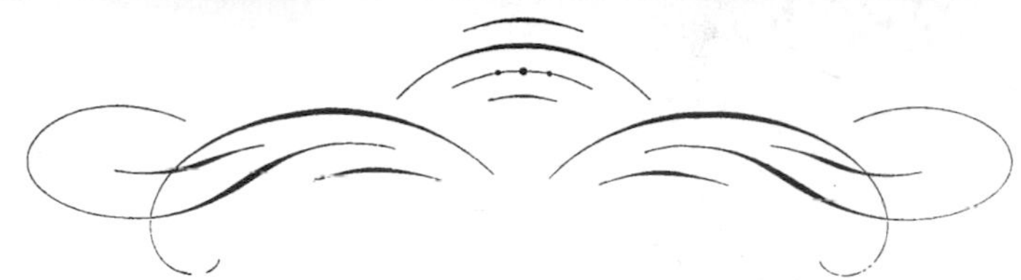

WEIRD AND WONDERFUL SNACKS (1): CHINATOWN

I love taking my friends on culinary adventures when they come over to play, so whenever I visit Chinese or Thai shops I keep an eye out for something new that might tickle their fancy. I picked up the selection in the photo opposite on a visit to London's Chinatown, but you can also find most of these online (see Suppliers, page 218). Wasabi peas are always great (they sometimes have quite a kick), and you can usually find all manner of sticky rice bun thingies, but the best fun is to be had when the packages aren't translated and you don't have a clue what you've let yourself in for!

INSTANT DIM SUM FUN

This is the epitome of lazy extraordinary food. We eat frozen ready-made dumplings at my house whenever we need an emergency feast, or when we've been so greedy over a weekend that there's nothing left in the fridge come Monday. Don't let the fact that they're frozen put you off—dumplings freeze really well, and they taste great. I keep a selection of them in the freezer: lots of basic shrimp, vegetable, pork, and chicken gyoza-style dumplings to fill me up and a few of the more delicate *har kau* open-topped ones for steaming.

The Cantonese phrase *dim sum* refers not to a specific food but to a way of eating. It translates as "close to the heart," and refers to any range of snacks and nibbles and tasters that you like. Dumplings are probably the most common, although chicken feet and duck's tongues are very popular, too.

There are two usual methods for cooking frozen dumplings: the delicate open-topped ones and the big fat buns just need to be steamed (usually for about 8 minutes or so), while the gyoza-style ones need to be very gently simmered from frozen first (the water has to boil very gently, otherwise the pastry casings can split), and then drained and finished off in a frying pan with some vegetable oil to brown them lightly. Check the instructions on the package, although be forewarned—they are often translated into English a little oddly. Serve with soy or ponzu sauce and eat with chopsticks.

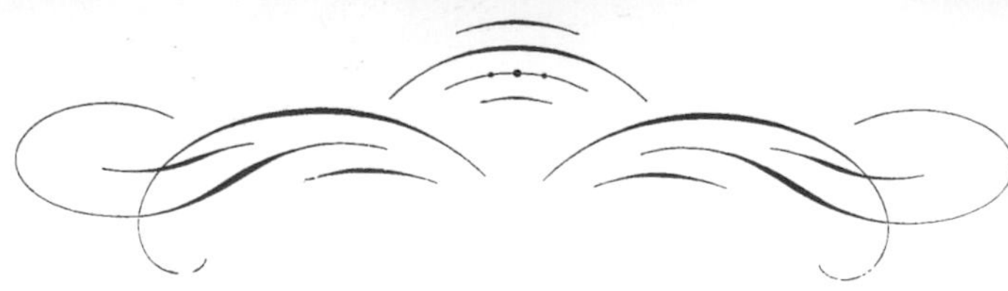

WEIRD AND WONDERFUL SNACKS (2): INSECTS

Insects are one of the world's great untapped food resources, and there's a good reason for that: most people are terrified of them. So why should you bother trying to overcome that fear to eat them? Partly because you will never forget the first time you ate a good roasted insect, whether you enjoyed the experience or not. And seeing as our lives are often made up of long periods of highly forgettable hard work and stress, scattered with occasional sparks of highly memorable excitement and joy, I think we should find any excuse to indulge the excitement and joy.

There's another, more vital reason to eat insects: the world's population is expected to grow from under seven billion now to nine billion by 2050, and the strain on food and land resources will mean that feeding those extra people on protein from animals will become extremely difficult. Insects, however, are doing pretty well: there are 40 tons of insect to every living human on the planet! Insects are healthy to eat, high in protein, and extremely efficient at turning vegetable matter into that protein. You're not convinced yet, I know, but when insect burgers are one-tenth the price of hamburgers...

The third reason to eat insects is simple—they can be really tasty. I've tried palm weevils in Cameroon; silk worm larvae in South Korea; Mopani worms in South Africa; bamboo grubs in Burma; maggots, cockroaches, crickets, and all sorts of strange and wonderful insectivorial flotsam and jetsam. I don't eat them to be macho; I genuinely want to discover enjoyable tastes and experience a little adventure in a mouthful. My current favorites are chapulines from Mexico—grasshoppers roasted in a little lime, chile, and salt—which are genuinely delicious when served with a beer.

Most insects are currently imported from countries where there's a long tradition of eating them—especially Thailand. I've cooked English woodworms and earthworms, and they're great, but hard to source in any great number. Insects really are a developing-world product. The products here are available online (see Suppliers, page 218) but mainly in small taster packages, so until everyone else joins the party, they will remain as a fun little snack to terrify and amuse your friends.

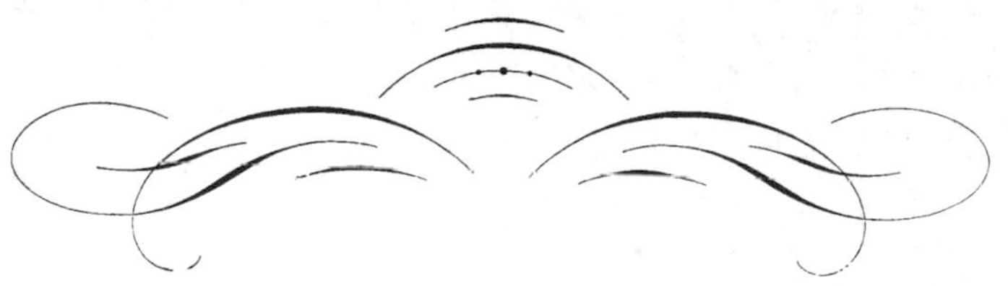

COCHINEAL

This isn't a recipe, it's a diversion. Because it just struck me that you probably thought you weren't an entomophagist (insect-eater), when the reality is that bugs crop up in our food whether we want them to or not. The US Food and Drug Administration allows up to 150 insect fragments in each ¼ pound of flour, in what amounts to an admission of the inevitability of their presence in our grub. Basically, anyone who eats natural food is likely to munch a few bits of bugs without ever thinking about it. And, of course, there's honey, which is, let's face it, bee-regurgitated nectar.

But bugs are often put in food as an ingredient, too. If you've ever eaten sausages, certain types of liquorice, M & Ms, or indeed a pink candy of any description, you are highly likely to have eaten the little crinkly purple thingies in the photo opposite. Those tiny fellas are dried cochineal bugs that I harvested and dried myself on a resurrected cochineal farm in Lanzarote, Spain (the industry is dormant on the island because South American countries now produce cochineal more cheaply). When you see "cochineal," "carmine," or E120 listed on the label of a food, what you've got is a tiny amount of those bugs ground into a pink or purple dye.

Cochineal bugs are little scale insects each about the size of a peppercorn, which grow on cactus leaves in Lanzarote and some South American countries, with the world's main commercial production in Peru. Thousands of acres are planted with cacti specifically for the purpose of cochineal production and the bugs look like gray, moldy, scrofulous carbuncles clinging to the cactus leaves as they grow. But under their gray covering, the bugs have a deep crimson-purple coloring, and when you crush a live one in your palm, it bursts with an explosion of deeply colored blood that's so intense that it stains your hands and clothes on contact.

Cochineal is popular with food manufacturers because it's an organic product (so it can be labeled "natural") and it's very stable, unlike some dyes that can often fade over time. It can be used as a simple ground powder of the dried insects, or a more intense extract called carmine, which is a dye made from chemically processed cochineal.

Facts about cochineal:
1. It takes between 70,000–100,000 bugs to make just over 2lb of dye.
2. France is the world's biggest importer of cochineal.
3. Cochineal currently costs $30–40 per pound.
4. You might think cochineal is a little weird. I think it's quite beautiful.

DIPS AND SPREADS

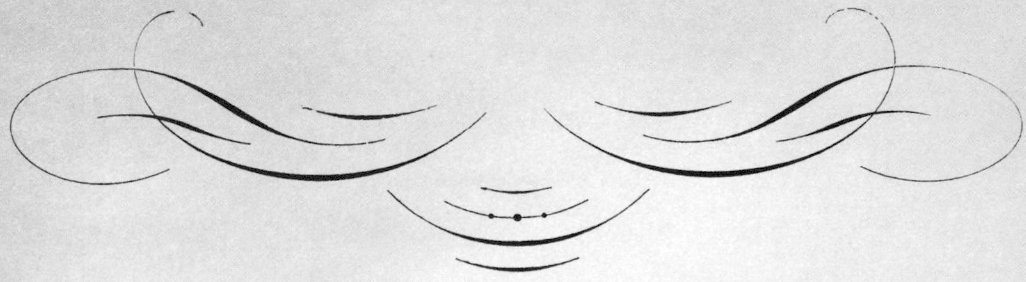

I HAVE ONE SMALL REQUEST: Please, please, please get your friends to make their own butter. While the dishes in this chapter are all fun, delicious, hands-on, shareable numbers that get people interacting with their food (even if it's just by spreading something delicious on their bread), I can't tell you how extraordinary the simple task of churning your own butter can be. There's something magical about this little act of creation that means your friends will never forget the experience—which is what we're up to here after all. Kids absolutely love making their own butter, but adults are invariably reduced to wide-eyed, childish delight by it, too.

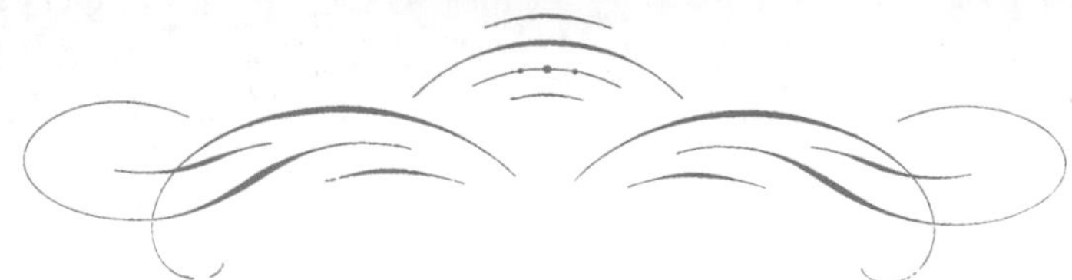

DO-IT-YOURSELF BUTTER WITH BREAD

There's a lovely sense of discovery in making your own butter, especially when you then spread it on bread and eat it immediately. I can't recommend this recipe enough—it couldn't be easier, and it's lots of fun.

Butter is simply cream or milk that has been churned until the watery buttermilk separates from the butterfat, and this is easily done by pouring some room-temperature heavy cream into a jam jar and shaking it for a few minutes. The buttery fat coagulates into a handsome lump in the middle of a pool of watery buttermilk. The buttermilk is drained away, and the remaining butter is ready for use. It tastes a little creamier than normal butter because you won't be able to extract quite as much buttermilk as the dairy can, but it's still delicious. If the cream is cold from the fridge it will still work, but it'll take a lot longer (10–15 minutes) and it will go through a disheartening whipped-cream stage that you may feel will never end!

The science of the whole affair is fascinating, and there are few better explanations of it than that by the brilliant Harold McGee in *On Food and Cooking*, should you care to take a look. He quotes Irish poet Seamus Heaney's description of butter as "coagulated sunlight."

SERVES 6

4 cups heavy cream, at room temperature
6 medium-sized jam jars, very clean
fresh crusty bread and salt, to serve

Give everyone an empty jam jar and have them add heavy cream until each jar is one-third full, then replace the lid. Tell your friends to shake their jars until the butter solids have separated from the buttermilk, which should take about 2–4 minutes. You can tell when it's ready because you'll feel it thumping as you shake your jar.

When the butter has been churned to satisfaction, place a bowl in the middle of the table with a strainer sitting in it, lined with a clean dish towel or piece of muslin. Have your friends pour the contents of their jam jars onto the dish towel, and leave to drain for one minute. After the watery buttermilk has drained away, you'll be left with butter. Take the dish towel by each of the four corners and bring them together over the bowl. Twist and squeeze to wring out any excess buttermilk.

Serve the freshly churned butter right away with some crusty bread—homemade would obviously be a joy—and some salt, for those who prefer salty butter.

Homemade butter will keep in the fridge for a week or so. It's good for cooking but not for frying, since the slightly higher water content may make it spit and burn in a frying pan.

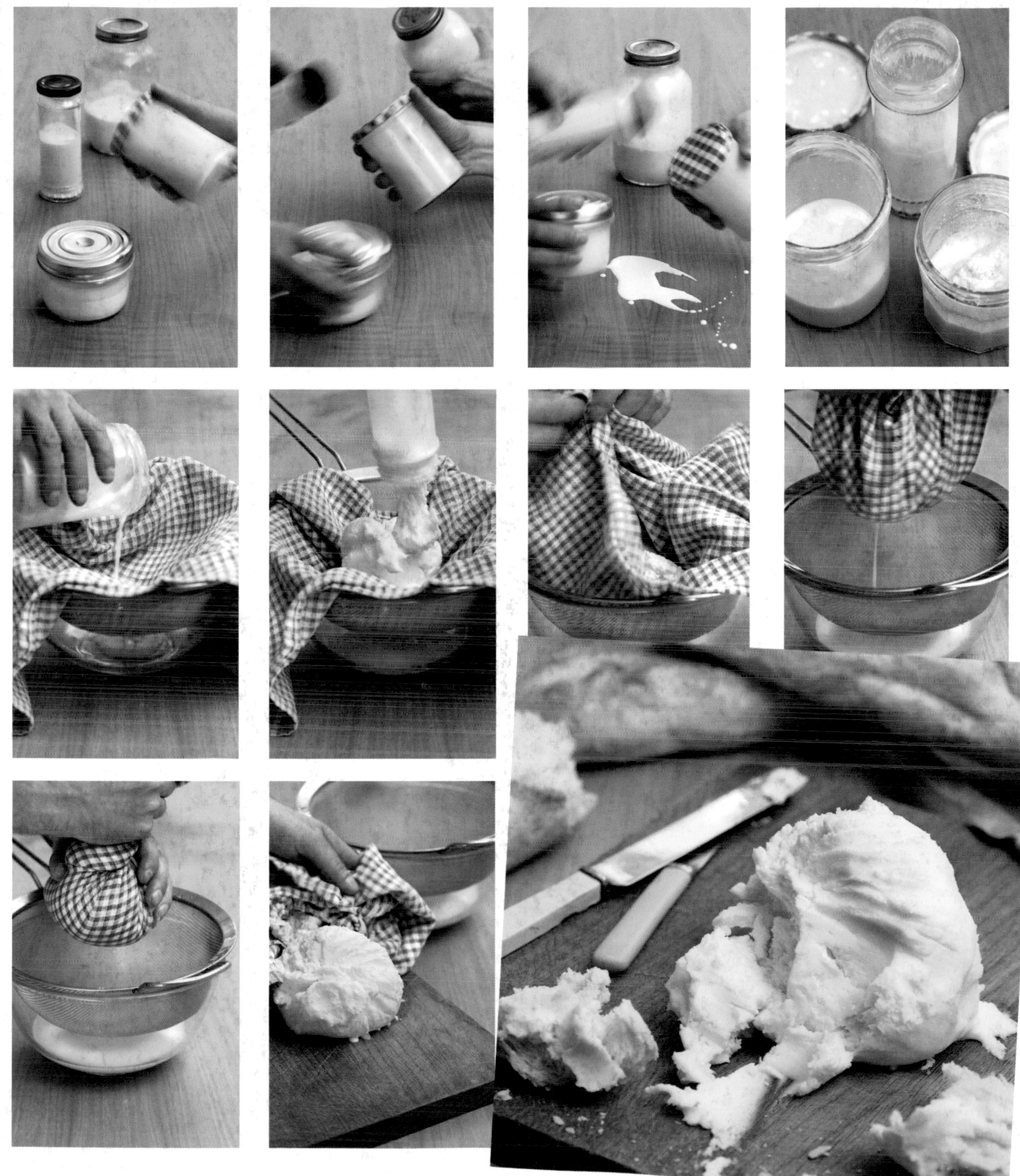

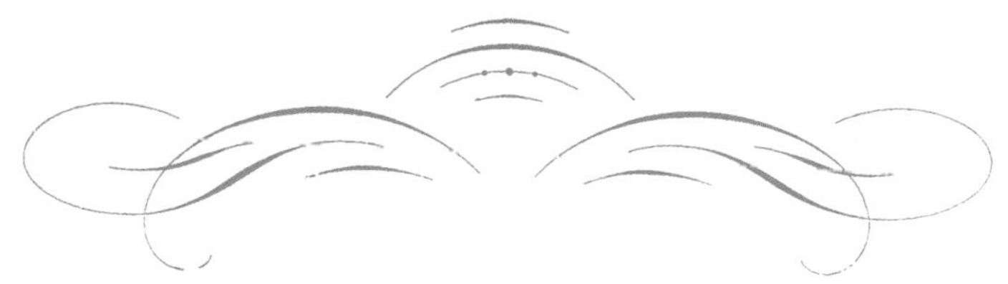

FLOWERPOT-BAKED BREAD

Terra-cotta flowerpots have been fired at very high temperatures in a kiln, so they can cope with being baked again to make little breads, and they also help to create a great crust. You can use pretty much any bread recipe for this—I've given you a basic white bread version, but you can try fruit ones, cheesy ones, or muffins.

If you want a shortcut to making your own bread dough (it does take a little application after all) and you own a breadmaking machine, you should be able to get it to do the whole dough making process and stop before the baking part. Then you just transfer the dough really carefully (so that you don't knock the air out of the dough) into the flowerpots and bake.

By the way, it's impossible to tell you how many flowerpot loaves this recipe makes—it all depends on the size of your pots! Make sure that they are unglazed and new, or at least very clean.

MAKES ABOUT 1¾LB

1 x ¼oz envelope active dry yeast
2 teaspoons sugar
3¾ cups white bread flour
(plus extra for kneading)
1 tablespoon salt
butter, for greasing

Put the yeast and sugar in a cup with a tablespoon of warm water and stir until dissolved. In a large bowl, stir together the flour, salt, and the dissolved yeast and sugar.

Measure 1¼ cups warm water into a measuring cup and slowly add it to the flour mixture, stirring continuously with a wooden spoon. Continue to add the water, a splash at a time, until you have a nice moist dough. (The exact amount of water required will depend on the type of flour you're using.)

Turn the dough out onto a large floured surface and start kneading it with your hands. (You'll find it easier if you cover your hands with flour before you start.) Push down and away at the dough with the heel of your palms, then roll and fold the dough. You'll need to push, shove, and manhandle the dough for a good 5 minutes, until it's smooth and elastic. Add more water if the dough feels dry and more flour if it feels too sticky.

Lightly oil a large bowl and place the dough in it, then cover this with plastic wrap and leave it somewhere warm for about an hour to prove and rise. After an hour, it should have doubled in size.

If your flowerpots have large holes in the bottom, place a piece of foil over them. Grease the insides of the pots very, very well, using lots of butter, then sprinkle a little flour over the butter.

Turn the dough out onto a floured surface and punch it down (this reduces the size of it again) by kneading it for another minute. Divide it up between your flowerpots so that the dough half-fills each one. Sprinkle a little flour over the dough in each pot. Cover the pots with a dish towel and leave the dough to rise again for another 45 minutes. Meanwhile, preheat the oven to 400°F.

Bake your bread in the oven. Small pots will need about 15–30 minutes, larger ones 30–45 minutes. You will have to keep an eye on them, since the cooking time will depend on the size of your pots. When the loaves are golden brown on top, remove them from the oven and place them on cooling racks to cool for 10 minutes or so before serving—in the flowerpots, of course.

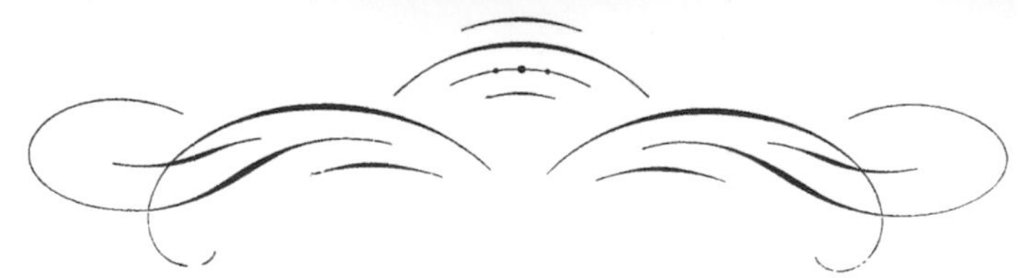

MAKE-YOUR-OWN BRUSCHETTA

The original idea behind these wildly popular Tuscan snacks was to show off the new season's olive oil harvest. Slices of hot toast were rubbed with garlic before being drenched in oil and sprinkled with salt. It's certainly a good way to make the flavors of olive oil sing, much like boiling new potatoes and pouring oil and salt over them while they're still steaming hot. (I'm terrible for snatching them right out of the pot before anyone else can get their hands on them.)

I love serving unmade bruschetta by putting all the ingredients on the table and letting everyone build their own. My friends can then play with the flavors they love best and it's fun to share ideas and to steal a nibble from the person sitting next to you. As with pizzas, you'll often find that less is more; resist the temptation to combine lots of ingredients, since you'll tend to drown out flavors. The classic combination is ripe tomatoes and basil leaves.

bread slices, preferably sourdough or ciabatta (toast on a grill pan, if you have one)
raw garlic cloves, halved, for rubbing on the bread
extra-virgin olive oil
sea salt

TOPPING SUGGESTIONS

- ripe tomatoes, roughly chopped and drained in a colander
- fresh basil leaves
- pitted olives
- mozzarella, torn into large pieces
- arugula leaves
- prosciutto (thinly-sliced dry-cured Italian ham)
- asparagus spears, blanched
- anchovies in oil
- balsamic vinegar
- Parmesan cheese (with a vegetable peeler for shaving)
- whole roasted garlic cloves (see right)
- tomato salsa (see right)
- roasted eggplant, zucchini, and/or peppers (see right)

Cut the bread into small slices and then toast them (on a grill pan, if you have one). Rub each slice with half a clove of raw garlic and then put the toasts on the table.

Choose a selection from the ingredients above and recipes (see right)—tomatoes and fresh basil leaves are must-haves—then serve them in bowls or plates. Encourage your guests to dive in, splash a large helping of olive oil over their bruschetta, sprinkle with salt, then choose from the variety of toppings.

ROASTED WHOLE GARLIC CLOVES

These make a wonderful bruschetta ingredient, but you can also keep them in the fridge to use in a pasta sauce, or for adding sparkle and wonder to gravies and stews. After the garlic has been roasted, you just squeeze a clove and a sweet, mild garlic paste will pop out of the end. This is great to spread right onto the bruschetta.

whole garlic heads
extra-virgin olive oil
salt and pepper
fresh thyme leaves (optional)

Preheat the oven to 350°F. Pull the papery outer skins off a head of garlic to allow access to the cloves. Place the head of garlic onto a piece of aluminum foil about 6in square, then pour some olive oil into the middle so that it seeps into the head. Sprinkle with salt and pepper and a few thyme leaves (if you have any). Pull up the corners of the foil and scrunch it into a pear shape. Roast for about an hour. Leave to cool a little before serving.

ROASTED EGGPLANT AND ZUCCHINI

Cut eggplant and zucchini into ¼in slices, then toss the slices in olive oil, salt, and pepper. Broil them on a ridged griddle pan until nicely browned.

Make more than you need, that way you have them to use later in salads or couscous.

TOMATO SALSA

1lb ripe, full-flavored tomatoes
5oz olives, roughly chopped
1 garlic clove, crushed
a handful of shredded basil leaves
balsamic vinegar
salt and pepper
extra-virgin olive oil

Roughly chop the tomatoes (no need to peel them), then leave in a colander for 10 minutes to drain away some of the juices and seeds. Put them in a bowl and stir in the chopped olives, crushed garlic, shredded basil leaves, a splash of balsamic vinegar, salt and pepper, and plenty of extra-virgin olive oil.

ROASTED PEPPERS

If you've ever wondered why roasted red peppers are so expensive at the delicatessen, I can confirm that it's because they are pretty tricky to prepare. I love doing this, but only when I'm not too pushed for time!

Cook whole peppers under a broiler, turning every 10 minutes until the skins are blackened all over. Wrap them in a plastic bag and leave to sweat for 15 minutes or so, then halve them, scrape the seeds out of the insides, and remove the skins with a flat knife. Save all the ugly but sweet, flavor-packed juices and mix them together with the peppers in a bowl.

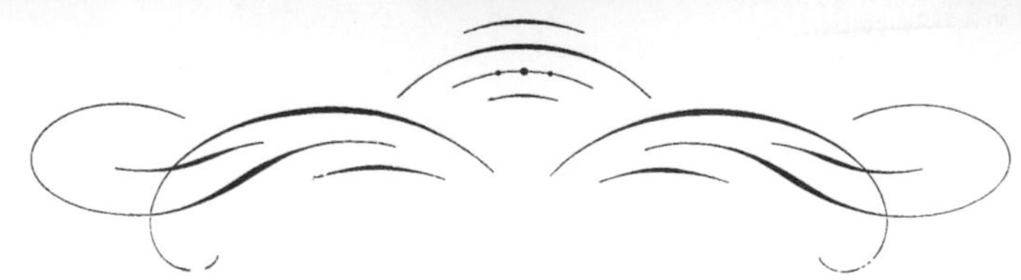

WHOLE BAKED VACHERIN CHEESE

This is an easy way to turn supper into a celebration. Vacherin is a raw cow's milk cheese that is sometimes sold wrapped in a thin band of spruce, and is packed in a circular wooden box. The packaging, and the fact that this superb cheese has a natural velvety crust concealing its creamy body, makes it perfect for baking into an extraordinarily easy and rich fondue. The best Vacherin arrives in my local cheese shop in late fall, so we eat this as a way of cheering and warming everyone up at the onset of winter.

SERVES 4 AS A MAIN COURSE

9½oz boxed Vacherin cheese, ripe and ready
¼ cup white wine (a fruity Gewürztraminer is fabulous for this)

FOR DIPPING
steamed baby new potatoes
chunks of crusty bread
blanched green beans
slices of good-quality cured ham, preferably Serrano
pickled gherkins

Preheat the oven to 350°F. Take the lid off the cheese, then wrap the sides and bottom of the box in foil without covering the top of the cheese. Poke a few holes in the crust with a fork, then pour the white wine over the top. Replace the lid so it sits loosely on top. Bake in the oven for 25 minutes.

Take the lid off the box, then slice off the crust (reserve it for munching though). Place the box in the middle of the table, surrounded by the potatoes, bread, beans, ham, and pickled gherkins. Encourage everyone to serve themselves by skewering a selection of ingredients to dip into the melted cheese.

MONS

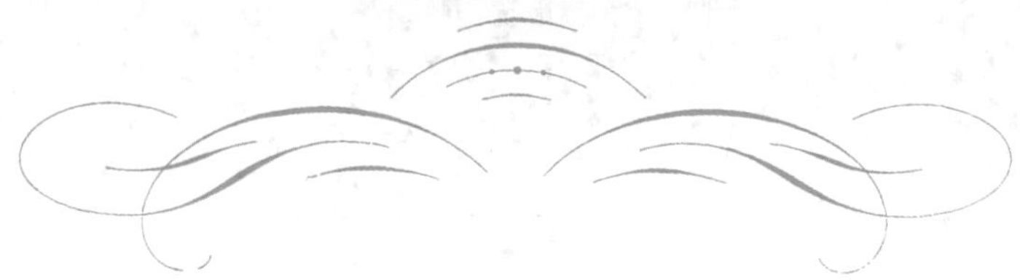

HEAD CHEESE: THE EASY VERSION

Sounds bizarre, but head cheese is also called "brains" and "brawn"—and it's a kind of pâté made from a pig's head. The French still call it *fromage de tête*, and you can buy veal or pig's fromage in most French markets. It is best cut into slices and eaten with pickled gherkins, mustard, and bread.

You can make an easy version of this or, if you like, you can make an absurdly complicated one. In my first book, *Gastronaut*, I indulged myself so much that I stretched the recipe out to eight pages. (It's the only recipe in the world that starts with the phrase "I'm rarely at home to Mr. Existential Angst, but…"), but the book you now hold in your hands is a practical cookbook, so here's the easy version. The recipe is still something of a project, since you need to brine the meat for a day first and you need to get up close and personal with a pig's head, which, if you've never done it before, is quite an experience. That said, there's nothing difficult here. It's an absurdly cheap dish, it's delicious, and, in my view, any usable part of a pig that ends up getting thrown away is a terrible waste.

Three hints: First, deal with your pig's head as soon as you bring it home—many fridges are too small to accommodate one, and at room temperature they spoil quickly. Second, don't forget that you'll need a pan large enough to contain the pig's head and more. Third, leave the window open when you boil the head; otherwise, the whole house will smell of pâté!

2 ¼lb salt
1 pig's head, ears removed and
  reserved (ask the butcher to do this, if you prefer)
2 pigs' feet (optional)
2 onions, peeled but kept whole
4 bay leaves
10 peppercorns
2 cloves (no more!)
1 teaspoon coriander seeds
a small handful of thyme
a large handful of chopped parsley
juice of ½ lemon

First, clean your pig's head. Remove any hairs, either using a razor or by burning them off with a blowtorch, and don't forget to clean the ears and around the snout thoroughly, too. Put the salt and 1 quart of water into a big pan (large enough to fit the pig's head, with room to spare). Heat gently, stirring until the salt dissolves. Then remove the pan from the heat, add the head, ears, and feet and pour over enough cold water to cover the head completely. Cover the pan with a lid and place somewhere cool for 24 hours.

Remove and rinse the head, ears, and feet, then drain and rinse the pan and replace the meat. Add the onions, bay leaves, peppercorns, cloves, coriander seeds, and thyme and cover with cold water. Bring to a boil, skim any scum from the surface, and reduce to a gentle simmer. Cook uncovered for about 4 hours, adding more water if the level drops to reveal the head. After 4 hours, the meat should be so tender that it falls off the bones easily.

Remove the meat from the cooking broth (reserving the broth) and set aside until cool enough to handle. Now for the icky part. Pull all the skin, meat, and fat off the head and ears and reserve. Pull out the tongue, peel off and discard the outer skin, and add the tongue to the rest of the meat. Now do the same with the feet, reserving the lovely unctuous bits, but rejecting any harder skin.

Chop the meat roughly and place in a bowl. Stir in the parsley and lemon juice and add a strained ladleful of the cooking broth to moisten it. Line a dish or two (a terrine dish would be great) with plastic wrap and add the head cheese mixture. Put a weight on top to compress it and squeeze out air, and refrigerate overnight to set. The head cheese will keep in the fridge for up to 2 weeks. Eat like pâté or fry it and serve with potatoes, French green lentils, and salad.

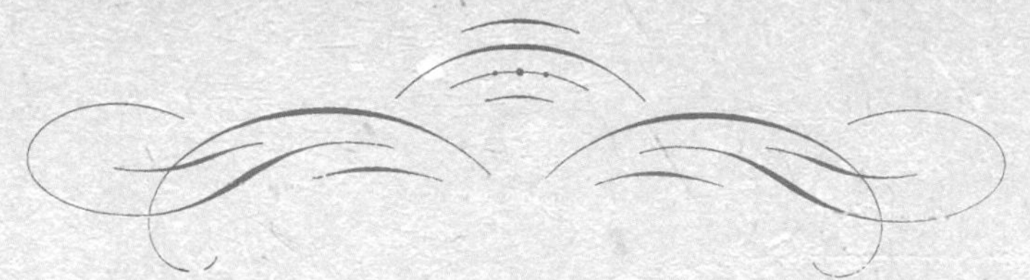

A LITTLE SELECTION OF FONDUES

Let's face it, fondues have received a lot of bad press. At some point in the Seventies, they got bundled together with the dropping of keys into bowls and—worse—sloppy ratatouille served as though it were the height of sophistication. But if you have a fondue set at home gathering dust, take a trip to the hardware store for a bottle of paraffin fuel and try one of these recipes (or indeed, the recipes for Bagna Càuda, Shabu-shabu, or Toffee Fondue: see pages 53, 128, and 202, respectively). Don't worry if you don't have fondue skewers—forks work just fine. If you have any fondue left over, don't throw it away—I use it as a fantastic sauce to go with fish or as a topping for baked potatoes, and it keeps surprisingly well in the fridge.

SPINACH FONDUE

SERVES 6

3lb spinach, thickest stems pulled off
3 garlic cloves, peeled and finely chopped
salt and freshly ground black pepper
large pat of butter
1 cup hard cider
1lb sharp Cheddar cheese, grated
2 pinches of ground nutmeg

TO SERVE
baby new potatoes, steamed or boiled
carrots, cut into sticks and blanched
cauliflower florets, blanched
broccoli florets, blanched
endive leaves, separated
radishes
1 large baguette, cut into bite-sized cubes

Wash the spinach, shake it well to drain, and put it into a large saucepan with the garlic, salt, and pepper. Place the pan over low heat and cook for about 6–8 minutes, stirring occasionally, until the spinach has wilted. Drain in a colander, pressing well to strain off the water (you need to get it really dry so the fondue isn't watery). Place in a food processor with a pat of butter and blend until smooth.

Bring the cider to a simmer in a fondue pan or heavy-bottomed saucepan. Reduce the heat, then mix in the cheese, stirring gently as it melts. Add the nutmeg and spinach, season, and stir to mix. Add a little more cider if the mixture feels too stiff.

You can prepare your dipping vegetables at this stage (see above), since the fondue will sit happily for a while, and it reheats very easily without spoiling the texture.

Place the pan of fondue onto a fondue warmer or camping stove on the table and keep warm, but try not to boil. Serve with the vegetables and bread cubes for dipping.

CHEDDAR AND CIDER FONDUE

SERVES 6

¾ cup hard cider
¾lb sharp Cheddar cheese, grated
1 tablespoon cornstarch, mixed into a paste with a few splashes of cold water
1 teaspoon English mustard
splash of Worcestershire sauce
freshly ground black pepper

TO SERVE
3 apples
juice of ½ lemon or lime
1 large baguette
baby new potatoes, steamed or boiled
carrots, cut into sticks and blanched
cauliflower florets, blanched
broccoli florets, blanched
radishes

Bring the cider to a simmer in a fondue pan or heavy-bottomed saucepan. Reduce the heat, then mix in the grated cheese, cornstarch paste, and mustard. Stir gently until all the cheese has melted and it becomes a nice sticky goo. Add the Worcestershire sauce to taste, then test the consistency by dipping a piece of bread into the fondue. Add more cider to water it down or more cheese to make it firmer, as you see fit and season with black pepper. Reduce the heat so that it doesn't boil, but keep the fondue warm until you're ready to eat.

Peel and core the apples, chop them into bite-sized pieces, and toss them in the lemon or lime juice to keep them from turning brown. Chop the baguette into thumb-sized pieces.

Place the pan of molten cheese onto a fondue warmer or camping stove and keep warm, but try not to let it boil. Serve with the prepared vegetables, fruit, and bread for dipping.

CRAB FONDUE

SERVES 6

8oz cream cheese
4oz Caerphilly or Cheddar cheese, grated
8oz crab meat (brown and white)
¼ cup white wine
juice of 1 lemon
a handful of fresh dill or parsley, finely chopped
splash of Tabasco sauce
splash of Worcestershire sauce

TO SERVE
2 apples
juice of ½ lemon or lime
1 large baguette
radishes
asparagus spears, blanched
cucumber, cut into sticks
carrot, cut into sticks, blanched
broccoli florets, blanched

Combine all the fondue ingredients in a fondue pot or heavy-bottomed saucepan and place over low heat. Stir as the cheese melts, until all the ingredients are well mixed. Check the Tabasco levels (it should have a definite tang of chile heat) and adjust, if necessary.

Peel and core the apples, chop them into bite-sized pieces, then toss them in the lemon or lime juice to keep them from turning brown. Cut the baguette into thumb-sized pieces.

Place the pan of crab and cheese onto a fondue warmer or camping stove to keep warm (but not hot or boiling). Serve the fondue with the prepared vegetables, fruit, and bread for dipping.

BAGNA CÀUDA

Roughly translated as "hot bath," *bagna càuda* is basically an Italian version of crudités. Instead of dipping your vegetables into delicate mayonnaise, you sink them into a piquant bath of garlicky, oily, anchovy stuff that has such a gutsy taste, it smacks of the primordial soup of life itself.

This provides all the wonderful communal experience of the cheese fondue without the... well... the cheesiness. Unlike a cheese fondue, where you're essentially using bread to scoop out as much viscous matter as you can, only a thin coating of the "hot bath" is needed here to provide all the necessary flavor. That said, it's a much runnier substance, so you can't really dip your vegetable into a saucepan in the middle of the table, otherwise it will drip everywhere! It's much better to give everyone a bowl of their own, so that they can serve themselves the bagna càuda a ladle at a time and grab vegetables as the mood strikes.

SERVES 6

FOR THE BAGNA CÀUDA

1 ¼ cups milk
12 large garlic cloves, peeled
25–30 canned anchovies in oil, oil reserved (this is about 3 small 2oz cans of anchovies; if you can only find salted anchovies, rinse them first)
½ cup, plus 2 tablespoons butter, diced
⅔ cup extra-virgin olive oil
⅔ cup heavy cream

FOR DIPPING, A SELECTION OF THE FOLLOWING:

baby new potatoes, steamed or boiled
radishes
celery, cut into large sticks
asparagus, blanched
radicchio or endive leaves
sweet potato, cut into long fries and roasted until lightly browned
baby carrots, blanched
red and yellow peppers, cut into long, thick slices
small baby artichokes, halved
crusty bread

To make the bagna càuda, pour the milk into a small heavy-bottomed saucepan, add the garlic cloves and heat the pan until the millk reaches a gentle simmer. (If you want a really garlicky sauce, crush the garlic into the milk and skip this simmering.) Cover the pan and simmer the milk gently for 8–12 minutes, until you can easily crush the garlic cloves into the milk using the back of a fork.

Add the anchovies to the garlic and milk and cook for another 5 minutes, until they disintegrate. Add the butter, olive oil, and reserved oil from the canned anchovies and stir until the butter starts to foam a little. Add the cream and heat until simmering, then remove the pan from the heat and gently whisk the sauce into a runny paste.

Arrange the vegetables on a large serving platter in the center of the table, give everyone a small bowl, and put the saucepan of bagna càuda straight onto the table (don't forget to put a heat-resistant mat down first), with a ladle so that your friends can serve themselves.

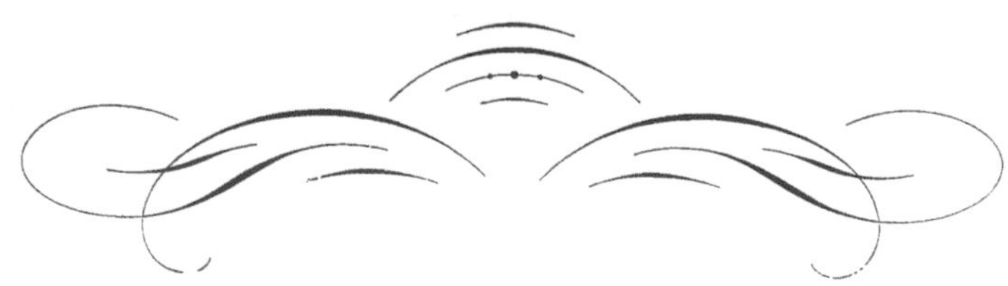

OUTRAGEOUSLY RICH CHICKEN LIVER PARFAIT

This is velvety smooth, rich, luxurious to the tongue, and strangely refined for something so cheap and simple to cook. I've tested lots of painfully complex parfait recipes, but they're so time-consuming to make that I've spent a fair amount of time over the last 10 years refining this one to achieve maximum unctuousness from minimum hassle. (By the way, don't try using whiskey instead of brandy, even if you're desperate. I know from bitter experience that it makes the parfait taste disgusting!)

MAKES 1LB, ENOUGH TO SERVE 10 AS AN APPETIZER

½lb free-range chicken livers
1 cup butter, preferably unsalted
1 cinnamon stick
pinch of freshly grated nutmeg
2 garlic cloves, crushed
2 fresh thyme sprigs
2 tablespoons brandy (or Calvados, for a nice twist)
1 teaspoon salt
1 teaspoon fresh thyme leaves
crusty bread, to serve

First, prepare the chicken livers. Pull off and discard any stringy bits, fat, and dark- or greenish-looking scraps, and gently cut or pull out any of the larger blood vessels that will come away easily.

Melt the butter in a heavy-bottomed frying pan until it is bubbling gently, then add the cinnamon, nutmeg, garlic, and chicken livers and cook over low heat for about 6–10 minutes, turning the livers once. Check them after 6 minutes; they should still be just pink in the middle, and not gray. Using tongs, remove the livers from the pan and place in the bowl of a food processor.

Add the thyme sprigs to the pan and put it back on low heat. Carefully add the brandy or Calvados and let it bubble away for about 4 minutes, or until the alcohol smell has gone, leaving just the brandy flavors. (If you're experienced in flambéing, turn the extractor fan off, turn the heat up to high, and carefully burn off the alcohol for 30 seconds.)

Remove the pan from the heat, discard the cinnamon stick and thyme sprigs, then carefully pour the contents of the pan into the food processor. Season with the salt and blend for 4 minutes, or until smooth and creamy. Pour the mixture into small bowls, coffee cups, or teacups for individual servings (or a large jar), scatter a few thyme leaves on top, and refrigerate for at least an hour until solid.

Serve with crusty bread and a good glass of hearty red wine.

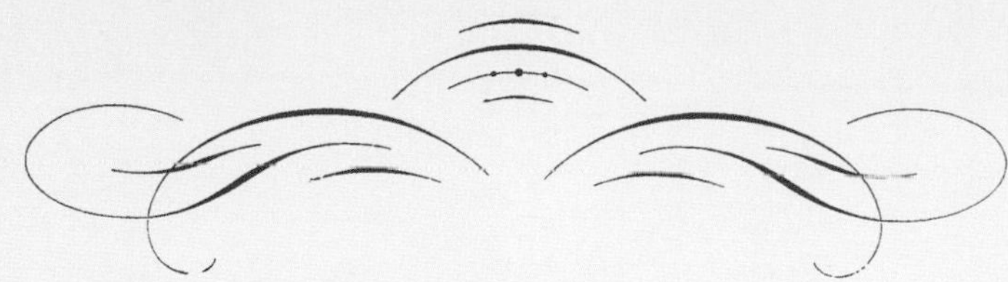

BONE MARROW ON TOAST

Bone marrow, championed by Fergus Henderson at his legendary St. John restaurant in London, home of great offal, is the very definition of unctuousness. I always keep veal bones in the freezer so that I can add them to stews for extra deliciousness and stickiness, and every now and then I can't resist roasting them and spreading the marrow on some good sourdough toast.

SERVES 6

12 fat pieces of veal bone, each about 2–3in long

TO SERVE
sourdough toast
lemon wedges
parsley leaves, finely chopped
sea salt

Preheat the oven to 350°F. Place the bones upright in a roasting pan and roast them for about 15 minutes, until the marrow inside is soft, shrinking a little from the bone around it, but has a light crust on top. Don't cook them for too long or the marrow will begin to melt away.

Serve the whole bones with the toast, lemon wedges, parsley, and salt. You'll need to offer teaspoons for your friends to use to dig out the marrow (the handle of the spoon often comes in handy), spreading it onto their toast and adding a squirt of lemon juice and a sprinkling of parsley and salt to taste.

3

SOUPS

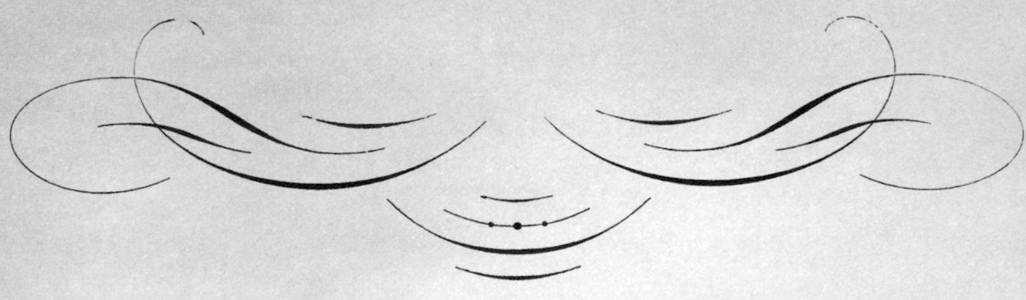

SOUPS ARE USUALLY THOUGHT OF AS homey, life-enhancing comfort foods rather than extraordinary flights of fancy. Well, it's time to turn these preconceptions on their heads with a few of my favorite spectacular liquid dishes. Of course, even the simple chilled soup can be turned into a journey of discovery if you serve it in an ice bowl or a pumpkin cauldron. But it's also lots of fun to serve people unusual food like nettles—if your friends have never eaten them before, they add a wonderful sense of drama and suspense to dinner. If they have eaten them before, you can revel in the fact that they don't tingle your tongue, and, instead, are both delicious and free. My only word of advice is that you keep the Windbreaker Soup away from any easily offended (or explosively flatulent) aged relatives.

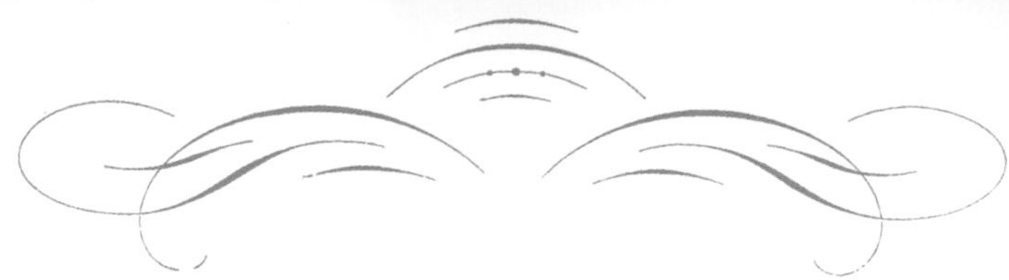

AVOCADO AND LIME SOUP IN AN ICE BOWL

Are ice bowls a celebration or an affectation? It's all in the delivery, really. If you're comfortable in your own skin and you love going to town to give your friends a night they won't forget, then go for it.

It's a pretty simple process. Basically, you pour some water into a large bowl, place another bowl into it with a weight on top, and then freeze. You'll need to make your ice bowl at least a day before you need it. The ice should set overnight, and it's just too stressful to make it on the day.

If you want something really spectacular, use distilled water, which tends not to cloud when frozen. You can add pretty much anything to the ice to decorate it: I've used everything from flower petals to Cadbury's Creme Eggs. For the one in the photo, I raided my daughters' toybox.

I'm a big fan of cold soups in the summer, and I love this zesty, shocking-green avocado-and-lime number, which reminds me of an exhilarating trip to Mexico. You need good ripe avocados for this.

SERVES 4

4 ripe avocados, peeled and pitted
2 garlic cloves, chopped, then mashed with ½ teaspoon salt
zest and juice of 2 limes
1 green chile, deseeded and finely chopped
1 quart vegetable or light chicken stock
2 handfuls of cilantro leaves and stems

Place the avocados, mashed garlic, lime zest and juice, chile, half of the stock, and all except a few sprigs of the chopped cilantro in a food processor and process until smooth. Pour into a large bowl and add the rest of the stock, then stir together.

Lay a piece of plastic wrap on the surface of the soup to prevent it from turning brown, then chill for 1–2 hours. To serve, pour into the ice bowl (if you've made one) and scatter the remaining cilantro on top.

TO MAKE THE ICE BOWL YOU WILL NEED:

1 large Pyrex or freezerproof bowl (this will need to fit in your freezer and will be the outer size of your ice bowl)
1 smaller Pyrex or freezerproof bowl (this will be the inner size of your serving bowl)
decorations—toy figures, flowers, or flower petals (optional)
water (distilled, if possible)

In the larger bowl, spread a layer of your decorations on the bottom and a little way up the sides. Put the smaller bowl on top to hold them there, then squeeze the rest into the gap between the bowls (this gap should be at least 1in thick). Put something heavy into the smaller bowl to hold it down, then pour water into the gap until it's full. Place in the freezer overnight.

Just before you're ready to use it, remove the bowl from the freezer, place in a sink of lukewarm water, and pour some lukewarm water into the inner bowl so that the ice bowl warms up and you can gently slip it out. Remember to place the bowl on a tray, since it will begin to melt, particularly if you're serving the soup outdoors in the sunshine.

IF YOU'RE USING FLOWERS OR SMALL DECORATIONS:
Put the larger bowl in the sink and fill it a quarter full with water. Add decorations, then float the smaller bowl on top. Place a small cutting board on top and push the smaller bowl down, until the cutting board lies flat on the surface, making sure that the inner bowl is right in the middle of the larger one. Check the decorations, then weight the board down with something heavy. Spill a little more water from the bowl (to make it easier to carry), then place in the freezer overnight.

LEA & PERRINS
CREAM SAUCE
LEA
vodka

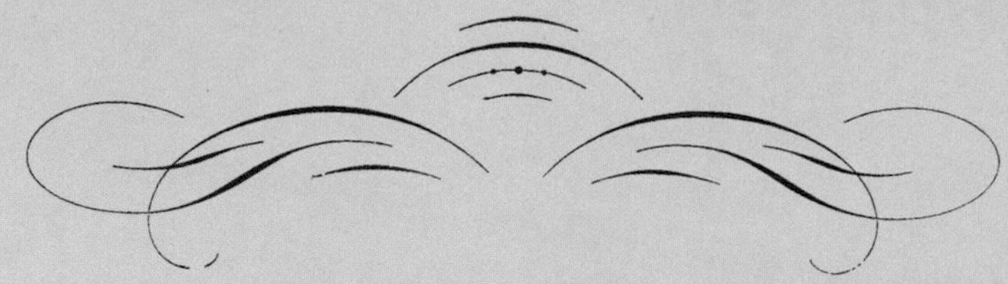

BLOODY MARY SOUP

I enjoy a Bloody Mary most when it's served on the bar semiprepared and accompanied by its little team of helpers: a bottle of Tabasco sauce, another of Worcestershire sauce, a little shaker of celery salt, and a celery-stalk stirrer. Such old-fashioned serving is rare these days, which is a shame, since I like to have control over my flavors, and offering guests a choice would seem like the decent thing to do when you consider that in the chile-heat department, one man's tongue-tickler is another man's Ring of Fire.

This rich and fiery soup is on a different planet than regular tomato soups, and it allows your friends to decide how hot they want it by providing the base soup but leaving the key flavoring ingredients on the table for them to add at will. If you wish, you can substitute the roasted tomatoes with cans of chopped plum tomatoes heated up with a tablespoon of sugar and perhaps some extra tomato paste, but the recipe below gives a wonderfully intense flavor.

SERVES 6

4½lb ripe, full-flavored tomatoes
3 tablespoons extra-virgin olive oil
2 teaspoons superfine sugar
salt and pepper
1 tablespoon sherry (or balsamic) vinegar
2 cups vegetable stock, warmed

TO SERVE
6 celery stalks
horseradish sauce
6 tablespoons vodka, (in individual shot glasses, if you prefer)
a small carafe of dry sherry
Tabasco sauce
Worcestershire sauce
salt and freshly ground black pepper
1 lemon, cut into 6 segments

Preheat the oven to 400°F. Halve the tomatoes and cut out the cores, then place them in a roasting pan with the olive oil, sugar, and salt and pepper. Toss them around to coat, then roast for about 30 minutes, or until they begin to brown.

Put the roasted tomatoes in a blender with the vinegar and process them until smooth, adding a little of the stock, if needed. Heat the stock in a pan, then add the puréed tomatoes and heat until simmering.

Serve the tomato soup in bowls, with a celery stalk in each. Place the rest of the ingredients on the table for your friends to create the flavorings they desire.

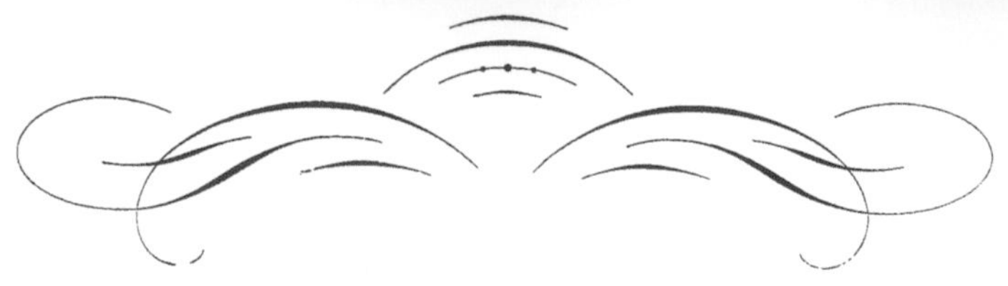

NETTLE SOUP

There's always a little frisson of fear when you put the first spoonful of nettle soup to your lips, no matter how many times you may have tried it. The sting is, of course, neutralized by boiling the nettles—although it's always more fun not to tell your friends and family this.

I think that nettle soup tastes a little like liquid grass—in a good way. It certainly has an uplifting effect, mainly because I only eat it in spring, just as summer is becoming a possibility once more. Be careful if you make this any later in the year; I've had several batches ruined by the bitterness of more mature nettles. You're really looking for new shoots that are only a few inches high. Make sure you collect them from an area that's unpolluted and unsprayed. Oh, and remember to wear gloves!

SERVES 4

a large carrier bag, packed with freshly picked, new-growth spring nettles
¼ cup butter
1 large onion, finely chopped
½lb peeled potatoes, roughly chopped
1 quart light vegetable or chicken stock (a good bouillon cube dissolved in water is fine)
salt and freshly ground black pepper
1 cup crème fraîche
fresh crusty bread and butter, to serve

Pick through the nettles and discard stems, flowers, and bugs. Wash the nettles thoroughly in cold water, then put them in a colander to drain. Melt the butter in a saucepan, add the onion, and cook over low heat until soft and golden. Add the potatoes and nettles and cook for another 10 minutes. Add the stock and bring to a boil, then reduce the heat and simmer gently for 15 minutes. Process the soup in a blender, then add salt and pepper to taste. Divide the soup between four warmed bowls, add a dollop of crème fraîche to each, and serve with bread and butter.

MELON, LIME, AND MINT SOUP

A perfect appetizer for a hot, sunny day: a cold soup served in the husk of the melon.

SERVES 6

3 ripe melons, chilled (Galia or cantaloupe are great)
1 cup orange juice
zest and juice of 1 lime
pinch of salt
1 teaspoon sugar
a handful of fresh mint leaves

Cut the melons in half, scoop out the seeds and discard. Shave a very thin slice from the underside of each melon bowl so that it will stand up firmly. Scoop the flesh out of the melons, leaving behind just enough for the bowl to stand (and being careful not to pierce the bottom).

Put all the melon flesh into a food processor with the orange juice, lime juice, salt, sugar, and half of the mint leaves and blend until smooth. If the mixture is too stiff, add a little more orange juice. Pour into the melon bowls.

If you kept the melons in the fridge, you can serve the soup right away. If not, refrigerate for about 30 minutes. Scatter the lime zest and remaining mint leaves on top just before serving.

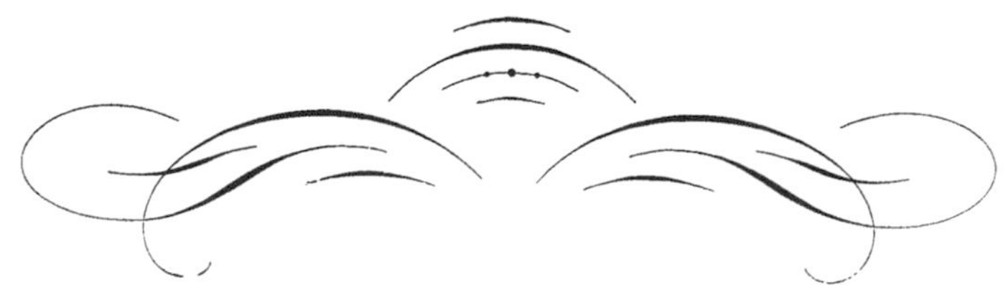

JERUSALEM ARTICHOKE "WINDBREAKER" SOUP

Jerusalem artichokes make a delicious soup and have a deep sweetness similar to globe artichokes, despite being entirely unrelated to them. But there are other, fruitier reasons for the inclusion of these vegetables in an extraordinary cookbook. Jerusalem artichokes are rampant little suckers on two fronts. First, I can't get rid of them from my garden, no matter how hard I try. I planted them about five years ago, and very abundant they were, too, despite the poor soil. After producing way more artichokes than we could eat or even give away, I tried to pull them out, but without success. Consequently, this may well be the most thoroughly tested recipe in the book.

Second, and more amusingly, Jerusalem artichokes are rampant when they're inside you, creating quite an astonishing amount of gas. It's thought to be due to inulin, a sugar that's hard to digest in your small intestine, but which the flora in your large intestine goes crazy for, breaking down with a whoop and a holler and producing lots and lots of gas in the process. You could see this as a disadvantage, of course, but gas really is an essential part of our digestion (if you didn't fart, you'd explode), and Jerusalem artichokes are a practical and dynamic way of explaining the workings of the digestive system, especially to kids, who love the effects. By the way, it may take a little while for the inulin to do its job—possibly not until your friends have gone home, which may be a blessing, depending on your point of view, and your love of *schadenfreude*.

SERVES 6

½ cup butter
1 large onion, finely chopped
¼lb carrots, peeled and roughly chopped
¼lb celery (or celery root), roughly chopped
1½lb Jerusalem artichokes, scrubbed clean (tough-skinned varieties should be peeled) and roughly chopped
1½ quarts chicken or vegetable stock (a good bouillon cube will do)
salt and freshly ground black pepper
1 cup crème fraîche

Melt the butter in a large heavy-bottomed saucepan, then add the onion, carrots, celery, and artichokes and cook over medium heat for 15 minutes, stirring frequently.

Add the stock, bring to a boil, then reduce the heat and simmer for another 15 minutes. Transfer to a food processor and blend in batches until smooth. Season with salt and pepper to taste, then pour the soup into warmed bowls, add a dollop of crème fraîche to each, and serve.

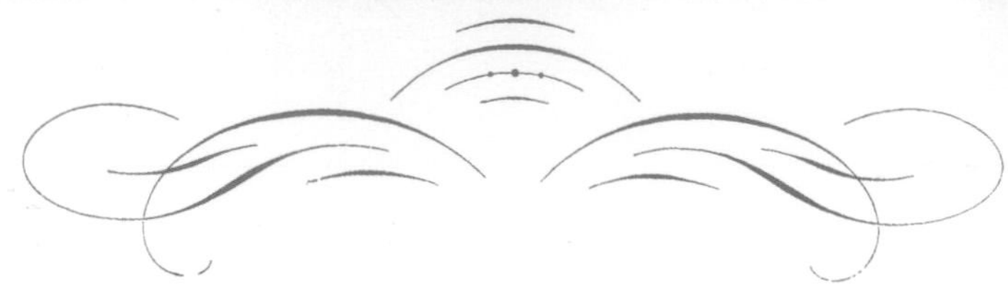

FRAGRANT PUMPKIN THAI NOODLE SOUP

This really is a fabulous use of a remarkable vegetable. The pumpkin's tough skin keeps the precious flesh inside fresh from the end of summer right through until spring, if stored in a cool, dry place, and that golden flesh yields a surprising depth of flavor and sweetness, especially when roasted, which makes it a great replacement for meat in pasta sauces.

One pumpkin yields so much flesh to eat that I thought it only fair to supply four recipes instead of just the one. You start by making this soul-meltingly delicious Thai soup, which you can serve in the hollowed-out pumpkin "cauldron." The next day you can cut the remaining pumpkin into pieces for roasting, and use it as a great accompaniment for roast lamb (or pot roast), in a salad, or in a rich pasta sauce (turn the page for the recipes).

SERVES 4

1 large pumpkin, weighing at least 9lb (or, if you don't want to serve the soup in a cauldron and use the remaining flesh for other recipes, 20oz pumpkin flesh)
1 large bunch of cilantro, stems finely chopped and leaves roughly chopped
4 big garlic cloves, peeled and roughly chopped
2½in piece of ginger, peeled and grated
½ red chile, finely chopped
2 tablespoons sesame oil
1 tablespoon vegetable oil
2 teaspoons Thai fish sauce (nam pla)
1 teaspoon ground cumin
3 lemongrass stems (outer leaves removed), finely chopped
6 kaffir lime leaves (optional)
13½oz can coconut milk
1 quart fish stock (or chicken or vegetable stock—boullion cubes are fine)
zest and juice of 1 lime
8oz dried egg noodles

Cut the top quarter off the pumpkin to make a large circular lid (you'll use the flesh from this to make the soup). Scrape out the seeds and stringy pieces from both parts of the pumpkin and discard them. Set the main piece aside (but do not refrigerate).

Cut some (but not all) of the flesh from inside the lid—you'll need about 1½lb—then cut it into small (1in) square chunks. Leave enough of the flesh on the pumpkin that it won't collapse when used as a bowl (use the rest for the next recipes).

Put the cilantro stems (reserve the leaves for garnishing), garlic, ginger, chile, sesame oil, vegetable oil, Thai fish sauce, cumin, lemongrass, and lime leaves (if using) into a bowl or mortar and process using a small hand blender or crush with a pestle until you have a paste.

Put a large heavy-bottomed saucepan on low heat and very gently fry the herb and spice mixture for 5 minutes. Add the coconut milk and stock to the saucepan and stir to combine, then add the pumpkin chunks. Bring to a boil, then reduce the heat and simmer gently for about 15 minutes, until the pumpkin is tender.

Add the lime zest and juice and the egg noodles and cook for another 4 minutes, or until the noodles are cooked. Pour the hot soup into the pumpkin cauldron and place on the table for serving. After use, rinse out the pumpkin cauldron and keep cool; use the flesh for the following recipes the next day.

3 MORE USES FOR YOUR PUMPKIN

ROASTED PUMPKIN

2lb pumpkin flesh, cut into thick slices
3 tablespoons olive oil
2 teaspoons coriander seeds, roughly crushed
2 teaspoons cumin seeds, roughly crushed

Preheat the oven to 350°F. Cut all the skin from the pumpkin. In a bowl, toss the slices in a few splashes of oil with the crushed coriander and cumin seeds, then lay them on baking sheets. Roast for about an hour, or until the pumpkin is gently browned. Eat with roasted lamb.

ROASTED PUMPKIN SALAD

If you still have a couple of pounds of roasted pumpkin left over, try this as an instant lunch: simply mix together a bowl of roasted pumpkin slices with a torn-up ball of mozzarella, some lovely ripe tomatoes, a handful of basil, a couple of spoonfuls of Greek yogurt, and a few splashes of extra-virgin olive oil.

ROASTED PUMPKIN AND LEMON TAGLIATELLE

2lb pumpkin flesh, cut into thick slices
6 garlic cloves, unpeeled
olive oil
a small handful of sage leaves, finely chopped
zest and juice of 2 lemons
salt and freshly ground black pepper
tagliatelle, prepared according to your liking
Parmesan cheese, grated, to serve

Preheat the oven to 350°F. Cut all the skin from the pumpkin, toss the slices and unpeeled garlic cloves in a few splashes of oil and lay them on baking sheets. Cover with foil and roast for about an hour, or until the pumpkin is nicely browned.

Squeeze the garlic from the cloves and put in a bowl with the roasted pumpkin, chopped sage, lemon zest and juice, a generous splash of olive oil, season with salt and pepper, and mash the mixture together. Mix into the cooked pasta, add grated Parmesan, and serve.

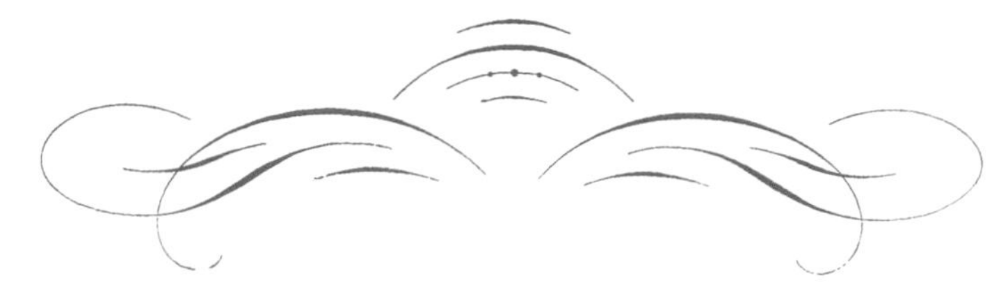

PAPPA AL POMODORO (LIQUID PIZZA)

This is a whopping great gutsy soup for a cold day when you feel in need of either some zip, or a big hug. Essentially, it's a tomato soup thickened with hunks of bread, and it's especially delicious made with sourdough—stale or not. The bread soaks up all the flavors and somehow melts into a sublime silkiness. I can't help thinking that it's essentially a liquid pizza. In a good way.

This is made with both canned tomatoes and some extra fresh tomatoes that you roast beforehand to give a really deep flavor.

SERVES 4

1lb ripe tomatoes, quartered*
8 tablespoons extra-virgin olive oil
1 teaspoon sugar
salt and freshly ground black pepper
4 garlic cloves, peeled and finely sliced
a handful of sage leaves,
roughly chopped
1 teaspoon chopped red chile (optional)
½lb bread—preferably sourdough
or ciabatta—torn into shreds
2 x 14½oz cans of tomatoes
salt and pepper
fresh bread and butter, to serve

* If you're pushed for time or you're making this in the winter when really good ripe tomatoes are hard to find, you can cheat by using an extra can of tomatoes and skipping the roasting.

Preheat the oven to 375°F. In a roasting pan, toss the fresh tomatoes in a splash of olive oil, the sugar, salt and pepper, and roast them uncovered for 20 minutes.

While the tomatoes are roasting, heat a large, heavy-bottomed saucepan and add 3 tablespoons olive oil, garlic, sage leaves (reserving some to use as a garnish), and chile (if using). Cook over low heat to soften them for a few minutes, but don't let them brown, then add the bread and toss it in the oil. Add the canned tomatoes and break them up with a wooden spoon. Fill one can with water and add that, too. Simmer for about 15 minutes.

Remove the tomatoes from the oven and stir them into the soup, along with any juices from the roasting pan. (Peel the tomatoes if you prefer them that way—I like the texture of them unpeeled.) Pour over another 3 tablespoons olive oil and check the seasoning (it usually needs salt) and consistency, adding some more water if necessary—it should have the texture of thin oatmeal. Stir again and simmer for 2 minutes more.

Pour the soup into warmed bowls and drizzle each with half a tablespoon of olive oil; scatter extra sage leaves over each bowl. Serve with bread and butter.

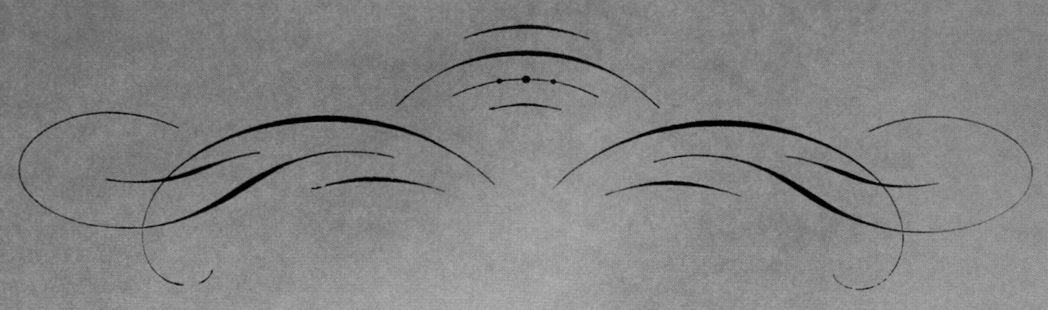

4

APPETIZERS

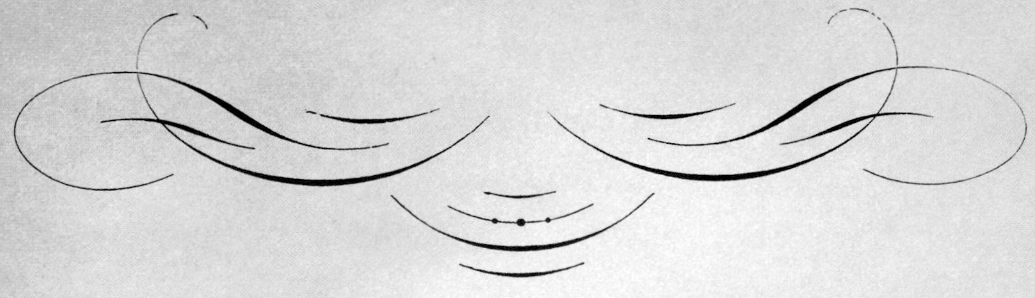

OKAY, HOLD ONTO YOUR HATS, because it's time to cut loose and play with some of the world's most wonderful, most extraordinary ingredients. Herein lie razor clams, frogs' legs, jellyfish, and stuffed zucchini blossoms. Obviously, some of these ingredients are more exotic than others, but it doesn't take much asking around or internet searching to lay your hands on anything here. If unfamiliar ingredients give you the willies, don't worry, because there are also some simple, cheap, and familiar foods in this chapter. Any butcher worth his chops will be able to get some veal bones for your bone marrow and even whole artichokes are a hands-on culinary extravaganza as long as you serve them as described here: whole and unadorned, rather than fancied up as a restaurant chef must, for fear of making a mess of the maître d's table linens.

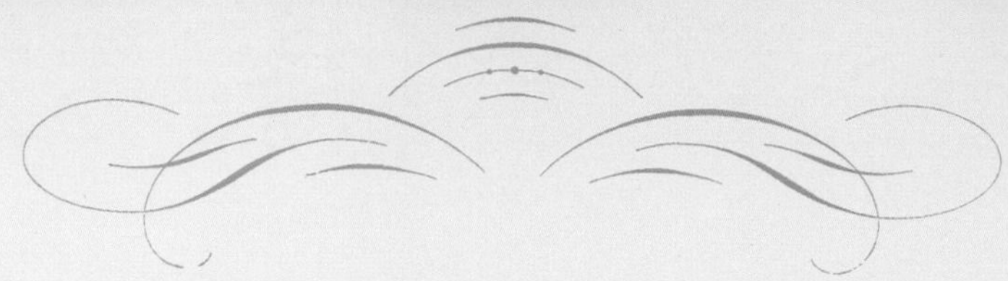

WHOLE ARTICHOKES WITH LEMON BUTTER

Eating whole artichokes is great, messy, interactive fun, but is it really that extraordinary? Well, that depends on your frame of reference. You're probably a hip, adventurous, sophisticated eater already, but I've found that even though lots of my friends have had prepared artichoke hearts in the past, the majority of them have never faced the whole shebang, leaves and all, before, and they're always excited when trying it for the first time. And, in case you haven't been introduced to these strange and wonderful vegetables, I'd be thrilled to do the honors.

PER PERSON:

1 large globe artichoke
¼ cup butter
salt and freshly ground black pepper
zest and juice of ½ lemon

Pull any straggly leaves off the artichokes, then chop off the thick stem. Bring a large pan of salted water to a boil, then add the artichokes. Bring back to a boil and cook for 20–25 minutes, checking after 20 minutes by pulling off one of the larger leaves in the middle. The base of the leaf (where it attaches to the core) should be soft enough that you can easily bite a little nugget of artichoke flesh from one side with your teeth. When they are ready, remove and place upside down to drain for 5 minutes, then place them upright on plates.

In a small saucepan, melt the butter with a large pinch of salt and pepper, add the lemon juice and zest, and pour over the middle of the artichoke so that it soaks in. Serve with a large bowl in the center of the table for the discarded leaves.

HOW TO TACKLE A WHOLE ARTICHOKE

Pull off the outer leaves one at a time, dipping each one in the butter and biting the little lump of tender flesh from the inside edge with your teeth before discarding. Keep going until you get to the tiny little leaves with no flesh in the middle (they are often purple and aren't really edible).

Using a knife, cut a bowl shape out of the middle of the artichoke, taking out the center leaves and the spikes that are underneath them. Throw this away and scrape any stubby pieces of choke from the middle, too. You will be left with a bowl-shaped section. This is the heart—the delicious central part that's so revered. Chop or tear it into chunks, dip in the remaining butter, and eat.

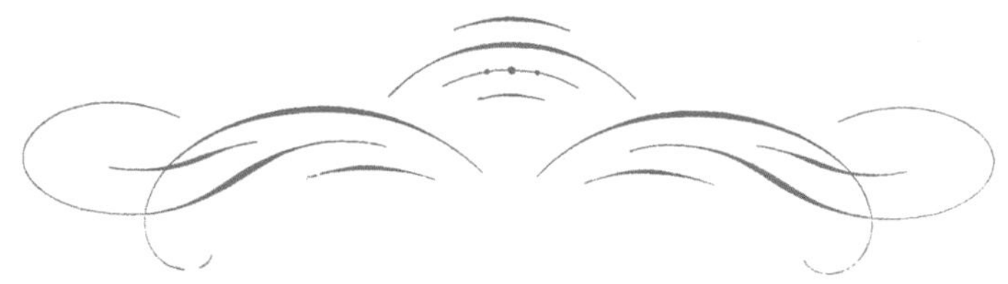

STUFFED ZUCCHINI BLOSSOMS

Zucchini blossoms are symbols of happiness and sunshine for me, partly because Georgia is the acknowledged house expert at making them (and, therefore, it's a love thing) and partly because they are strictly seasonal, so when they are available it must be summer. They aren't always easy to find, but they do crop up at farmers' markets, although the best place to get them is right out of your own garden, since they wilt quickly after picking. My mother very kindly gives me hers. If you ever get to a market in the south of France, you'll often find a stall selling them remarkably cheaply.

When you get your blossoms home, keep them cool and use them soon, otherwise they'll wilt. There are a few different recipes for them, but basically you'll need to remove the stamens of the blossoms and then stuff them with a creamy combination of cheese, herbs, and lemon, then dip them in a batter and fry them. Georgia's favorite stuffing is actually brandade de morue (a pâté made with salt cod mixed with a little rosemary). I love making my own brandade, but it does take a long time, so try this more achievable recipe first and see if you enjoy it.

SERVES 6

7oz ricotta cheese (or brandade, if you have some)
2 tablespoons grated Parmesan
zest of 2 lemons
1 tablespoon lemon juice
1 tablespoon fresh thyme leaves
salt and freshly ground black pepper
18 zucchini blossoms, zucchini still attached, if possible; stamens removed
vegetable oil, for frying

FOR THE BATTER
1 ½ cups all-purpose flour
1 egg yolk
1 ¼ cups beer or water
pinch of baking powder

In a bowl, mix together the ricotta, Parmesan, lemon zest and juice, and thyme, and season to taste with salt and pepper.

Make a tempura batter by mixing together the flour, egg yolk, beer, and baking powder in a bowl, and stir it to combine. Don't worry about making it smooth—the classic tempura batter is actually quite lumpy.

Using a teaspoon, very carefully fill each zucchini blossom with the stuffing mixture. Press the ends of the blossoms around so that they seal the filling in. Don't worry if they split a little, and don't worry about making them immaculate.

Fill a large pan with oil to a depth of around 1 ¼ in (or use a deep-fat fryer, if you have one) and put it on medium heat. The oil is hot enough when a small chunk of bread dropped in it browns within a few seconds. Dip each zucchini blossom in the batter, then place carefully into the oil a batch at a time, and fry until golden. When the blossoms are nicely browned, remove and lay them on paper towels for a few seconds to drain off any excess fat, then sprinkle with salt and serve immediately.

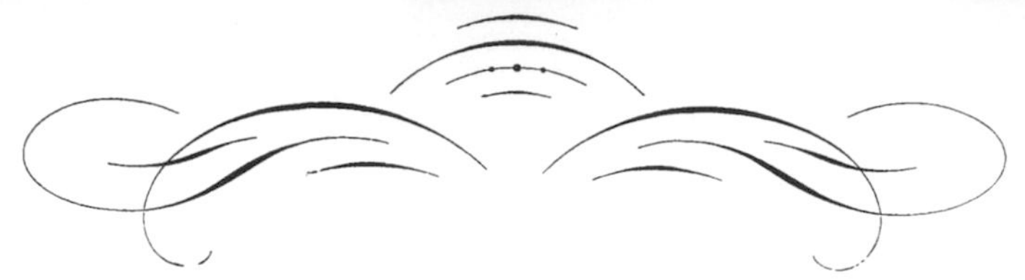

FLOWER SALADS

You've probably heard of edible nasturtiums, but there's a surprising variety of other flowers that are good to eat, too. You can add them to salads, or make entire flower dishes, like the one below. I love borage, elder flowers, and dandelions, in particular, and I'll grab a few roses when Georgia isn't looking, but I've always thought it is a terrible shame that buttercups are poisonous. You should remove greenery and the pistils and stamen from most flowers before you eat them.

Be sensible when choosing blossoms to eat—for example, picking wildflowers is fine on public land, but if you're on private property, you should get permission to pick flowers from the owner and not trespass. Make sure, too, that you only use blossoms that you know haven't been sprayed with a non-food-grade pesticide. For these reasons, it's probably best to avoid curbside flowers. In case you want to experiment with other flowers, here's a brief and incomplete guide to some interesting flowers that are edible and some that aren't:

EDIBLE

● borage (great in gin and tonic) ● chives ● dandelions ● elder flowers ● primrose and evening primrose ● scented geraniums (petals only) ● hollyhocks ● lavender ● rosemary ● roses (petals only—remove the light-colored "heel" from the base of each petal) ● marigolds (petals only) ● nasturtiums ● chrysanthemums (petals only)

NOT EDIBLE

● anemone ● lily of the valley ● foxglove ● ivy ● hyacinth ● iris ● daffodils ● buttercup ● mistletoe ● wisteria

DANDELION AND ELDER FLOWER SALAD

You can eat the entire flowers of elder flowers and both the flowers and leaves of dandelions, so this is a particularly good combination. Dandelions have a sort of bittersweet taste and elder flowers, which flower in late spring to early summer, are just sublimely sweet and floral-tasting.

2 large handfuls whole dandelion flowers, cut off as close to the flower as possible, all stems and green parts from around the neck removed
9oz dandelion leaves, washed (use arugula, if you can't find these)
2 large handfuls of elder flowers, checked for bugs, and pick off the stems

FOR THE DRESSING

1 tablespoon orange juice
1 teaspoon walnut oil
1 teaspoon white wine vinegar
salt and freshly ground black pepper

Put the dandelion flowers and leaves in a bowl. Combine the dressing ingredients together in a small bowl and mix thoroughly. Pour over the salad and toss together, then scatter the elder flowers on top.

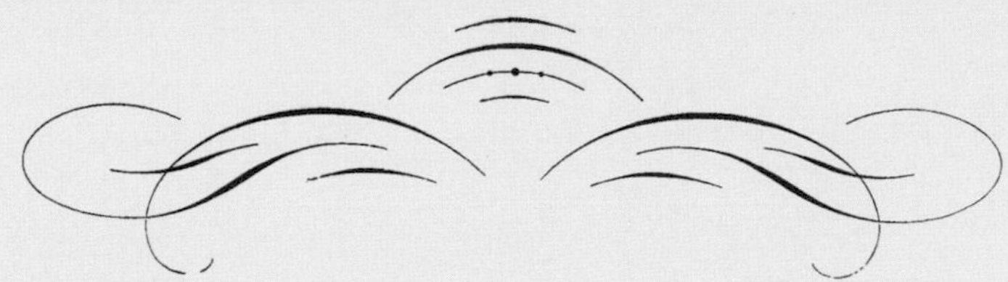

CLAMS WITH LINGUINE (LINGUINE ALLE VONGOLE)

You can make this recipe with pretty much any type of clam: palourde, telline, littleneck, or even the modest cockle. In Britain and the States, cockles don't get the respect they deserve. Vast amounts are gathered from British sands, tickled out from where they hide, happily filtering plankton from the seawater. They are fabulous, and very cheap—but three-quarters of British cockles are exported to Spain and France, where they are revered. When it comes to eating mollusks, smaller is often better, since smaller mollusks are less chewy. The same holds true for littleneck clams (also known as steamers); when you are choosing littlenecks to eat, look for the small guys, rather than going for the biggest you can find. And don't forget the unassuming cockle when making this recipe.

The experience of eating clams in pasta is a wonderful journey in its own right, as you ferret around for the little shells before gnawing out their precious meat and getting your fingers deliciously flavored for licking. The one thing you need to be really careful about is washing them: cockles can carry a fair amount of sand, and there's nothing quite as annoying as a gritty lunch.

SERVES 6

18oz dried linguine or spaghetti
¼ cup extra-virgin olive oil, plus extra for splashing
6 fat garlic cloves, thinly sliced
½ red chile, deseeded and finely sliced
a large handful of parsley leaves, finely chopped
2¾lb cockles, or other clams, thoroughly washed
2 tablespoons white wine
salt and freshly ground black pepper

Boil the pasta until just *al dente* (no more, since it will need to stand for a few minutes while you do the next bit), then drain and return to the pan, toss in a few splashes of olive oil, and cover the pan to keep it warm.

Put a large saucepan over medium heat, add the olive oil, garlic, and chile, and gently fry for 2–3 minutes, until the garlic starts to soften but not so miuch that it turns brown.

Add the parsley, cockles, wine, salt and pepper, and stir through. Cover the pan; continue to cook for 5–6 minutes, shaking the pan gently, until all the cockles have opened.

Add the drained pasta, stir through, check the seasoning, and serve. You'll need a bowl in which to throw the empty shells, and some napkins for wiping sticky fingers.

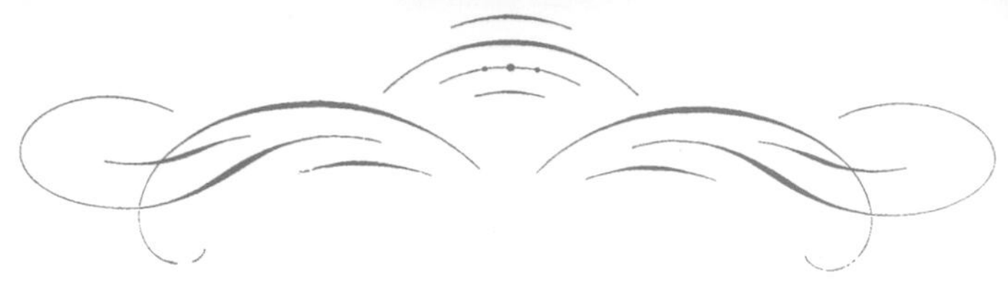

APPLE CAVIAR

I'll be straight with you here: For most of this book, I have gone to huge lengths to make sure that all the flights of fancy and extraordinary recipes and techniques are easy, practical, and achievable, using ingredients that you can find at your local supermarket. This recipe is different.

This is a fantastic, fun recipe, and its fascination lies in the scientific intricacy of an intriguing arm of molecular gastronomy known as spherification. You can buy the strange-sounding ingredients (and even a starter kit with all the supplies for this recipe) online from a company called Trufflina™ (see Suppliers, page 218), which provides great chefs with weird and wonderful specialized odds and ends. You specifically need sodium alginate (which helps turn liquids into thick gels) and calcium chloride (which hardens the outer shell of the gel on contact, creating the caviar effect). You'll also need a syringe to use as a very exact dropper (available from pharmacies or as part of the starter kit) and some digital scales that read amounts down to 1g.

SOME USEFUL TIPS

- Read the recipe carefully and buy or gather all your ingredients before trying it out.
- This recipe might not work with very hard tap water (although I've never had any problems with London tap water, which is very hard indeed!) If you have hard water, you might be better off using bottled mineral water or distilled water.
- The calcium chloride works best if your base juice is a little acidic, like apple, orange, or black currant, so if you are tempted to try other flavors, check them out first. Also, very high sugar solutions sometimes won't work.
- Don't be tempted to reduce the juice to a syrup in an attempt to make the flavor stronger, since this may unbalance the reaction and your caviar might not set. You need a high free-water content (i.e., not too sugary) in your base syrup to begin with.
- Once you have the hang of it, you can do the final part at the table, should you like a bit of theater.

1 cup apple juice
3g sodium alginate
20g superfine sugar
5 drops green food coloring (or other color)

FOR THE CALCIUM BATH
2 cups water
5g calcium chloride
10 drops green food coloring (or other color)

FOR STORAGE
1 cup apple juice
a few drops of green food coloring (or other color)

Pour the apple juice into a bowl. Mix the sodium alginate and sugar together in another bowl, then slowly add it to the juice a little at a time while whisking it (do this in an electric food mixer, if you have one) trying to keep it from turning lumpy. Add the food coloring and whisk gently for 5 minutes on the slowest setting, then leave the mixture to stand for 10 minutes as it thickens to a lump-free gel.

Make up the calcium bath in a bowl by mixing the calcium chloride and food coloring into the water and stirring until dissolved. Pour the apple juice (for storage) into a bowl and set aside.

Draw the gel into a syringe and, holding the tip of the syringe 4in above the bowl, squeeze it slowly to drop regular, steady drops into the calcium bath. Gently stir the water as you do this to help the drops turn into spheres.

The little balls of "caviar" shouldn't stay in the calcium bath for more than 3 minutes, or they will solidify too much. After each syringe-full, scoop them up with a strainer or tea strainer, rinse in cold water, then store in the bowl of fruit juice, adding a few drops of the food coloring to match the color of the caviar (otherwise the color will slowly fade). The caviar will keep for 2–3 days in the fridge.

Serve the caviar as a topping for pâté or soft cheeses, or to give an extraordinary twist to a sushi or sashimi party. It makes an extraordinary garnish for pork chops, too.

VARIATION: BLACK CURRANT CAVIAR
Replace the apple juice with black currant juice, made up to double the normal concentration, and use purple food coloring instead of green. Great with turkey.

VARIATION: ORANGE CAVIAR
Replace the apple juice with orange juice (the kind without pulp), use orange food coloring instead of green, and add 2 drops of orange oil (optional). Great with roast duck.

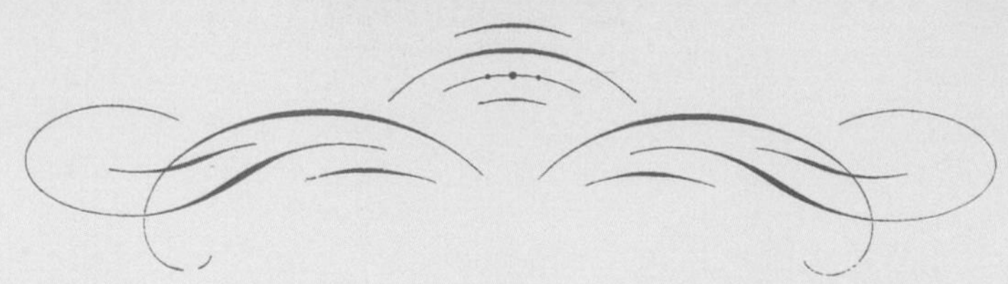

HOOLIGAN SQUASH WITH A CREAMY, HERB FILLING

I haven't made this name up—hooligans are small squashes, about the size of a fist—so just the right size for an appetizer. I love these because when you serve them whole, with their lids replaced, it's like you're handing out little presents to all your friends. In addition to being sweet and quirky, they are useful if you are feeling lazy or pushed for time, because you can cook them in the microwave in just five minutes. They do, of course, taste much better slow-roasted, because the flesh sweetens as it caramelizes, but microwaved ones still make a quick, fun supper. You scoop the flesh out with your spoon before eating the skins themselves (if you've oven-roasted them). Try different fillings: a teaspoon of harissa, grated sharp cheese, or just sour yogurt and a squeeze of lemon.

Like pumpkins, hooligan squash will keep for up to six months in a cool place (50°F is a pretty good temperature, although I usually just leave them outside the back door in a box). So when you see them in the supermarket, snap them up by the bucketload and store them for later use.

SERVES 6

6 hooligan squash (or other small squash)
salt and freshly ground black pepper
olive oil

FOR THE FILLING
4oz goat cheese (or feta or other soft, crumbly cheese)
8oz crème fraîche
2 teaspoons fresh thyme leaves
juice of ½ lemon

Preheat the oven to 325°F. Wash the squash, then pat dry, and carefully cut a small lid off the top (be careful—the skin is tough and they can slip around). Scoop out the seeds with a teaspoon and discard. Lay the squashes in a roasting pan and season the insides with salt and pepper. Put 2 teaspoons of olive oil inside each one before popping the lids back on. Roast for 1½ hours, or until the skins are just starting to brown (if you're pushed for time, you can roast them at 350°F for 1 hour, but they seem to taste better when roasted slowly).

Remove the squashes from the oven and set aside to cool a little while you make the filling. In a mixing bowl, crush the cheese a little using the back of a fork, then add all the remaining ingredients, and mix together. Check and adjust the seasoning to your taste, then remove the lids from the squashes, divide the filling between each of them, and replace the lids to serve.

THE MICROWAVE METHOD
Prepare the squashes as above, but put 1 tablespoon of olive oil inside each one. Put the lids back on and microwave each squash for 5 minutes on maximum power. Serve them just as they are, or add the filling.

Boreopacific gonate squid
Max size 25cm
Architeuthis dux
Giant squid
Max size 1500cm
Nautilus pompilius
Emperor nautilus
Max size 20cm

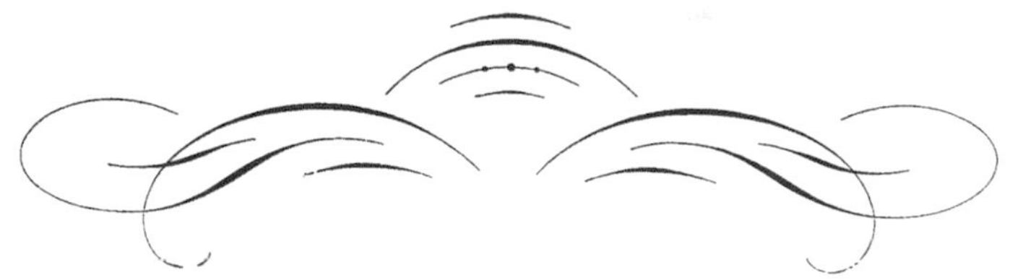

CRISPY JELLYFISH AND BEANSPROUT SALAD

Jellyfish are one of the world's great untapped food resources (another is insects, see page 34), and they are in abundance in the oceans, so eating them doesn't harm biodiversity. And if you've ever been stung by one, here's your chance for a bit of revenge.

Edible jellyfish are neither jellylike, nor do they sting. In fact, they are relatively fat-free and taste-free, so you eat them for their high protein content and their extraordinary texture, which is both rubbery and crunchy at the same time. You can buy them from many Chinese and Thai supermarkets and they come in two versions: "Jellyfish Salad," which is ready to eat, and "Salted," which has been preserved in salt and needs to be soaked for 3–4 hours before use.

I'm determined to find more uses for jellyfish, but I've been unable to crack new recipes. I tried jellyfish ice pops, but they didn't catch on, and I even spent several days trying to perfect a recipe for jellyfish burgers. I did finally manage it (the recipe's on my website at www.thegastronaut.com) but they were annoyingly complicated. If you come up with any new uses, I'd love to know about them. In the meantime, stick to this salad — it's great!

SOME JELLYFISH FACTS

1. A jellyfish has no brain and no central nervous system, with the exception of the box jellyfish, which has four independent brains. (I'm in awe; imagine ordering dinner at a restaurant when you have four brains!)
2. They are ninety-five percent water and five percent protein.
3. The *Turritopsis nutricula* jellyfish seems to be the only immortal being on the planet; it has the ability to rejuvenate itself when it becomes an adult. Weird, huh?

SERVES 4

FOR THE SALAD

6oz packaged, "ready to eat" jellyfish salad
6oz beansprouts
1 carrot, peeled and finely shredded
1 celery rib, washed and finely sliced
a small handful of cilantro leaves, roughly chopped
2 scallions, finely sliced

FOR THE DRESSING

1 tablespoon vegetable oil
1 teaspoon Thai fish sauce (nam pla)
1 teaspoon toasted sesame oil
1 teaspoon lime juice
½ teaspoon red chile, finely chopped

Put the jellyfish in a colander and rinse with cold water, then set aside to drain. Combine all the salad ingredients in a large bowl.

Put all the dressing ingredients in a lidded jar and shake well to mix them together. Make sure the jellyfish is dry, then add to the salad, pour the dressing over the top, and toss everything together.

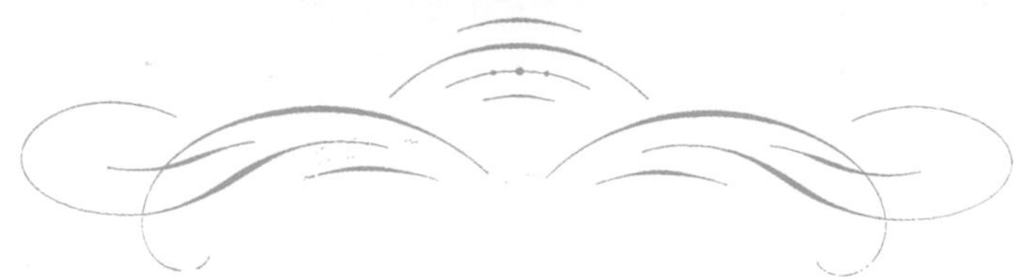

PINTS OF SHRIMP WITH LIME AND CILANTRO MAYONNAISE

This is a bit embarrassing really: a recipe that involves no cooking whatsoever, a tiny amount of preparation, and precious few dishes to do, yet there's a little interactive spectacle to it and it's delicious to boot. Doesn't get much better than that, does it?

Of course, the idea of serving a pint of shrimp is stolen wholesale from the traditional British pub lunch, where the publican doesn't want to put himself to the trouble of cooking—with all the gear, skills, and accompanying costs that requires—when he can simply have some good-quality shrimp and mayonnaise on hand in the fridge, make a tidy profit, and keep his customers happy at lunchtime.

You can, of course, make your own mayonnaise to fancy this up a little, but, if you don't have the time, a jar of good-quality, store-bought mayo and some nice bread from the bakery will do just fine. Serve your shrimp in pint glasses (bowls just don't seem to have the same effect) with some plates or bowls for shells, and watch everyone tuck in.

SERVES 4

2¾lb good-quality, sustainably sourced cooked shrimp, shell-on
zest and juice of 2 limes
a handful of cilantro leaves, finely chopped
¾ cup mayonnaise (see the recipe on page 121 if you want to make your own)

TO SERVE
brown, whole wheat, or soda bread and butter
some salad: tomatoes, radishes, cucumber slices, and carrot sticks—whatever's in season

Divide the shrimp into four pint glasses. Stir the lime zest and juice and the chopped cilantro into the mayonnaise and spoon this into four bowls.

Serve a pint of shrimp and a small bowl of mayonnaise to each person, with some salad and plenty of bread and butter that they can help themselves to.

As a variation, you could beat a little wasabi into the mayo for that fiery horseradishey kick.

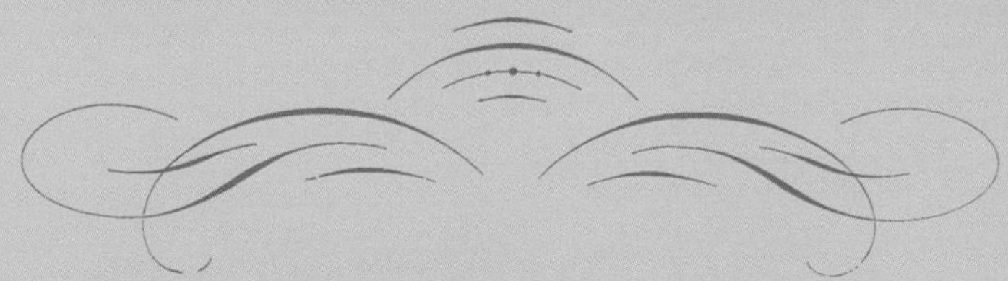

SALMON CAVIAR TAGLIATELLE

This spectacular dish is delicate and full-flavored, yet needs little planning and is simple to cook. Salmon eggs in jars last for about a year in the fridge, so it's worth keeping some on hand for when inspiration strikes. You can also make this with lumpfish caviar, which is cheap and also delicious, although it lacks the luxuriousness of salmon. Don't add extra salt (without tasting first), since the salmon and the eggs are both salty.

SERVES 4 AS AN APPETIZER OR 2 AS A RICH MAIN COURSE

9oz tagliatelle or fettucine
¼ cup butter
a handful of parsley, finely chopped
6oz crème fraîche
1 tablespoon lemon juice (one good squeeze should do it)
4oz smoked salmon, cut into thin ribbons
2oz salmon caviar (or lumpfish caviar)
freshly ground black pepper

Cook the pasta in a large pan of boiling water until it's *al dente*. Drain (reserving a cupful of the cooking water), return to the pan, add half of the butter, and toss to combine. Cover the pan to keep the pasta warm.

In a large frying pan, melt the remainder of the butter over low heat, then add the parsley, crème fraîche, and lemon juice and stir through. Turn the heat off, then add the pasta and smoked salmon and toss it through the creamy mixture until thoroughly coated. Add a few splashes of the pasta cooking water *only* if it seems too dry, then add half the salmon caviar, and mix very gently.

Serve on warm plates, topped with the remaining caviar (otherwise it all falls to the bottom) and some freshly ground black pepper.

CEVICHE OF SALMON AND BREAM

This is real wake-up food—a zesty, refreshing dish of thin slices of spanking-fresh fish marinated in citrus juice. It's not heated in any way, but neither is it, strictly speaking, raw (the citrus juices "cook" the fish by denaturing and coagulating the proteins—essentially, this is what happens when salmon is pan-fried). It's a burst of South American sunshine packed with a wonderful combination of flavors: lime, lemon, orange, cilantro, chile, and a little hit of ginger and Thai lemongrass thrown in for good measure. If you could have this for breakfast, it would be a perfect way to start the day, clearing away fuzzy-headedness and blasting your olfactory bulb through with the fresh air of anticipation.

When you make this, please don't be tempted to overmarinate the fish, since the citrus juice is a beguilingly powerful cooking tool: I'd leave it for an hour at the very most, and 10–15 minutes should be about perfect. Just make sure your fish is good and fresh. You can use almost any combination of fish, although salmon and white fish seem to work best. Scallops are excellent, as are pollack, sea trout, and lemon sole. Buy small fillets of whatever looks best at the fish counter and whatever was landed most recently.

SERVES 6

1 ¼lb mixture of very fresh salmon, sea bream, or other white fish fillets (filleted weight), pin-boned and skinned
1 tablespoon cilantro leaves, thinly sliced

FOR THE MARINADE
zest of 1 lime, 1 lemon, and ½ an orange
juice of 3 limes, 2 lemons, and 1 orange (blood orange, if in season)
3 tablespoons extra-virgin olive oil
1 fennel bulb or 3 celery ribs, very thinly sliced
3 scallions, very thinly sliced
2 lemongrass stems, outer leaves removed and very thinly sliced
½ medium hot red chile, deseeded and thinly sliced
1 tablespoon freshly grated ginger
½ teaspoon sugar

Make sure you prepare all the ingredients as listed before you start, since the fish should stay in the fridge until the last minute.

Put all the marinade ingredients in a jam jar or non-metallic bowl and mix thoroughly to amalgamate the flavors. Stir until the sugar has dissolved.

Cut the fish into the thinnest slices you can manage—ideally, they should be slivers as thin as a quarter. You'll find it easiest if you start with a freshly sharpened knife and cut at an angle so the knife rests against the fish.

About 30 minutes before you are ready to serve, take six dinner plates and put a spoonful of the marinade on each one as a base layer, making sure that you have at least half the marinade left over to cover the fish. Lay the fish slices on the little pools of marinade, mixing up the different fish and overlapping the slices. Pour the rest of the marinade over the top of the fish and pop them in the fridge for 15 minutes or so (no longer than an hour).

To serve, remove the plates from the fridge and scatter the cilantro over the top. Serve with some crusty bread for sopping up the juices.

RAZOR CLAMS

Razor clams are beautiful and extraordinary, and, occasionally, they can look a bit naughty. They are also becoming more common at fish markets and in restaurants, and it's about time, because they are sweet and delicious when cooked right—i.e., quickly and simply. The best I've ever tasted were at The Drapers Arms pub in Islington, London, and this is pretty much how they were cooked.

SERVES 6

½ cup butter
a splash of olive oil
6 garlic cloves, finely chopped
24 razor clams, thoroughly washed in lots of water to remove sand
a handful of fresh parsley, finely chopped
lemon wedges, to serve

Heat a wide, heavy-bottomed pan over medium heat and add the butter, olive oil, and garlic. Fry the garlic gently for 2–3 minutes, then turn the heat up and add the clams, turning them very gently in the butter so that they don't break. Fry them for 2–4 minutes, or until they all open. Don't cook for any longer than is absolutely necessary, since they turn rubbery if overcooked. Serve on warm plates, spoon the pan juices over the top, and scatter the chopped parsley over everything. Serve with the lemon wedges, bread, and butter.

FROGS' LEGS

One of the great rules about food is that the golden combination of butter, garlic, parsley, and salt will scatter culinary stardust on pretty much any fish or meat, and quite a few vegetables, too, come to think of it. I don't think that's the only reason that frogs' legs are so delicious, but it certainly doesn't hurt. They make for good eating and taste like very dainty chicken. And, of course, I'd be remiss if I didn't acknowledge that there's a frisson of *something* when you eat a frog.

You can often buy frozen frogs' legs at fish markets (despite the fact that they aren't fish), and they are readily available online, too (see Suppliers, page 218). If you find yourself in France, it goes without saying that you'll find them in the freezer section of most big supermarkets, marked as "grenouilles."

SERVES 6

2 tablespoons olive oil
18 frogs' legs, defrosted from frozen and dried thoroughly
4 fat garlic cloves, peeled and finely chopped
¾ cup all-purpose flour
salt and freshly ground black pepper
⅓ cup butter
a handful of fresh parsley leaves, finely chopped
lemon wedges, to serve

Put the olive oil in a large bowl, add the frogs' legs, and toss until thinly coated. In another bowl, mix the chopped garlic with the flour and plenty of salt and pepper. Toss the frogs' legs around in the flour until thoroughly coated.

Melt the butter in a large saucepan and fry the frogs' legs, six at a time (otherwise they'll cook too slowly and end up chewy), over medium heat, until they are nicely browned and crispy on the outside.

Drain each batch on paper towels to remove excess oil, then season again with salt and pepper to taste, and scatter with parsley. Serve with an arugula salad and slices of lemon.

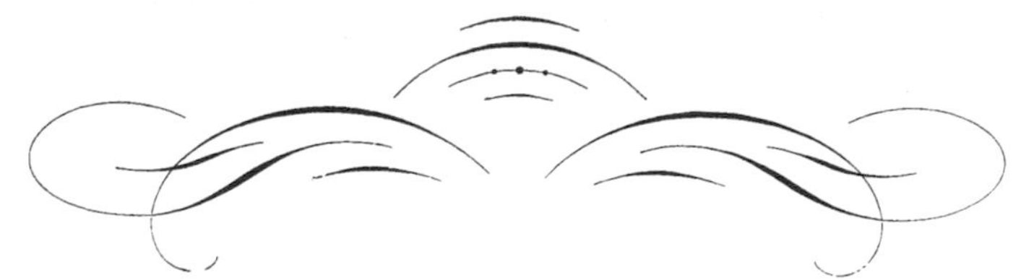

SWEETLY SPICED CHICKEN LOLLIPOPS

This is an unashamedly kid-friendly version of chicken drumsticks that my little girls adore, not just because the word "lollipop" makes them absurdly excited (the girls, not the drumsticks), but also because the lollipops are sweetly, stickily delicious. And, in fact, there's a good culinary reason for this method: When you take the skin off chicken, you allow better access for the marinades to flavor the meat. The lollipoppiness of these comes from the way you turn the skinned drumstick half inside out, leaving a handle to hold as you eat the marinated ball of chicken at the other end.

I've included a recipe for a delicious, fragrant teriyaki-style marinade, but you could use a ready-made bottled marinade, or even just a bottle of sweet chile sauce to pretty good effect. I particularly love a hot smoked paprika and garlic version (just mix with lots of olive oil and lemon juice), but it's got quite a kick for young palates, so we'll stick to the milder version here.

MAKES 8 DRUMSTICKS

8 chicken drumsticks, skinned

FOR THE MARINADE
2 garlic cloves, crushed
2in thumb of ginger, peeled and grated
2 lemongrass stems, outer leaves removed and very finely chopped (optional)
zest and juice of 1 lime
¼ cup honey
¼ cup soy sauce
¼ cup vegetable oil

Preheat the oven to 400°F. Preparing the drumsticks is a little tricky the first time you try it, but just imagine you're turning them inside-out like a sock. Take a skinned drumstick and, using a small knife, cut and scrape away the meat from around the bone only at the thick meaty end, then push the meat up toward the thinner end and over the knuckle. It should remain still attached to the knuckle. Don't worry about making them look pretty.

To make the marinade, combine all the ingredients in a bowl and mix together with a fork. Place your drumsticks in a bowl small enough for them to fit snugly, meat end down, then pour the marinade over the top. Cover and refrigerate for at least 20 minutes, and preferably 2 hours or longer.

Wrap some foil around the bones so they don't burn, then turn the drumsticks in the marinade one last time and place them on a baking sheet. Roast for about 40 minutes (depending on the size of your drumsticks), checking them twice to make sure they haven't dried out, and basting as needed.

While the drumsticks are roasting, pour the remaining marinade into a small saucepan and simmer for 2 minutes to make a dipping sauce, adding a splash of water if it seems too dry.

Check that the drumsticks are cooked through, then take out of the oven, remove the foil, and leave to cool for about 10 minutes, until they can be held comfortably without burning little hands. Serve with the dipping sauce.

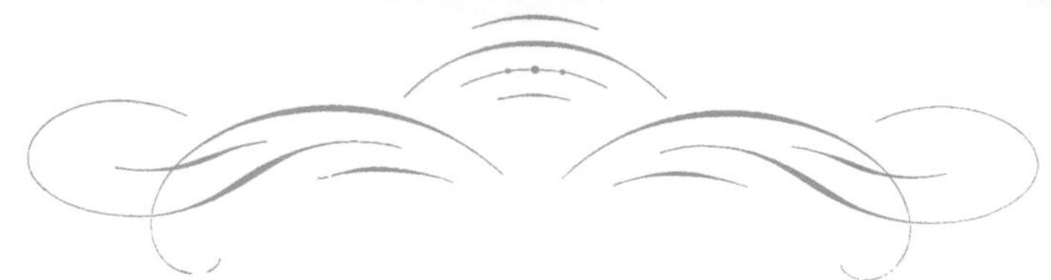

STICKY-SWEET CHICKEN HEART SKEWERS

This recipe is here because it's easy, cheap, and delicious, not to shock or test your friends' appetite for adventure—if you want to push them to their psycho-gastronomic limits, you'd be much better off serving them the Lambs' Testicles (see page 96).

Chicken hearts are absurdly cheap. So absurdly cheap that a heart from the finest organic, hand-stroked, and lovingly crafted free-ranger you can lay your hands on will still cost you less than a drumstick from any miserably caged bird. They are thumb-sized mouthfuls of very lean meat that need little preparation, and they don't taste in any way offal-like. I serve these to kids all the time and tell them that they are eating chicken nuggets. I don't think that's wrong of me, mainly because nuggets of beautiful lean chicken are exactly what they are. Duck or rabbit hearts are good, too, but they are more difficult to find.

SERVES 6

18oz free-range chicken hearts (if they have any suetlike fat near the top, don't remove it—it will help to keep them juicy)

FOR THE MARINADE
- ¼ cup honey
- ¼ cup soy sauce (or 2 tablespoons Worcestershire sauce)
- 2 tablespoons vegetable oil
- 2 scallions, finely sliced

Soak 12 wooden skewers in cold water for about 10–15 minutes. If you are broiling using a ridged grill pan, check that the skewers will fit. Cut them down with a sharp knife if they are too large.

Drain the hearts of any blood and pat dry. Using a sharp knife, cut halfway into each heart so that you can spread it out like a book. Thread the hearts onto the presoaked skewers so that they stay splayed out, and then lay them in one layer on a baking sheet or roasting pan.

In a jam jar or bowl, stir together the honey, soy sauce, and vegetable oil (don't worry if the oil doesn't blend properly). Pour this marinade over the skewers and turn them so they are completely coated. Set aside in the fridge for at least 15 minutes, and if possible for 2–3 hours.

Turn the skewers to coat them once more in the marinade, then heat a ridged grill pan (or broiler or barbecue) to high heat and cook the skewers until gently browned on both sides. This should take only 4–8 minutes in total, but check that they are cooked through before serving.

Meanwhile, heat the remaining marinade in a small saucepan until it boils, then reduce the heat and simmer for 60 seconds. Pour the sauce over the cooked skewers (or serve it in a bowl as a dipping sauce), scatter the sliced scallions over them, and serve on their own or with some salad and bread.

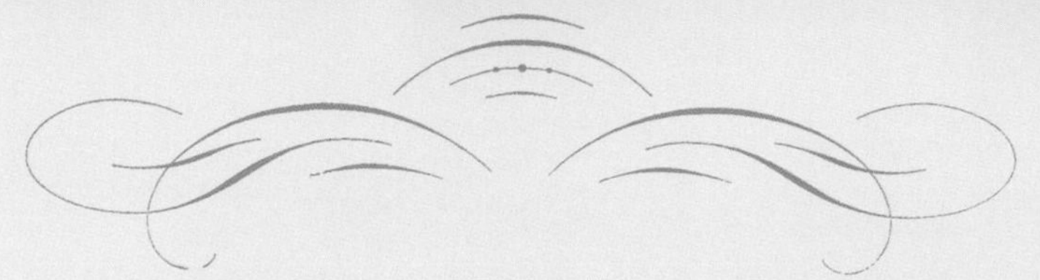

LAMBS' TESTICLES

I get quite evangelical about trying new food. After all, someone had to make some huge leaps in experimenting with cocoa to end up with chocolate. (Have you ever tasted raw cocoa or cocoa nibs? They're horrible!) And even the potato started off as an odd, wizened little tuber that was originally though to be inherently evil. We have a responsibility to the world to come up with some sort of solution to our food problems, so we must continue to experiment and explore.

I'm not sure if testicle-eating will solve the world's food problems, but it will probably help. They are delicate (similar to sweetbreads, although the myth that sweetbreads *are* testicles is untrue—see the recipe on page 159) and delicious and it would be a tragedy if protein of this quality were thrown away. In the past, I've followed complicated recipes for soaking and blanching them for hours, but after downing more than my fair share of nuts over the past few years I've realized that none of that is really necessary. I just peel them of the outer membrane (come on, now, be bold) and then cook them in the holy culinary trinity; butter, garlic, and parsley.

You can ask your local butcher for lambs' testicles, or look for them in supermarkets in ethnic areas where lamb is very popular. I'm very lucky to live in an area of London that has lots of Turkish stores, and the butchers often stock lambs' testicles very cheaply (you have to ask for lambs' "eggs," oddly enough).

SERVES 6

4 lambs' testicles
½ cup all-purpose flour
4 garlic cloves, peeled and finely sliced
1 teaspoon salt
freshly ground black pepper
¼ cup butter
2 tablespoons olive oil

Using a sharp knife, cut the testicles in half lengthwise, then pull the thick membranes off, together with any veiny bits at the end. The first one will be tricky, but you'll soon get the hang of it. You'll reveal a soft and light-pink interior. Discard the membranes and cut the soft interiors into chunks the size of your thumb.

In a large bowl, mix the flour, garlic, salt, and a few generous grinds of black pepper. Add the testicles and toss them around in the flour until well coated. (They may start to seem sticky, but that's fine.)

Heat the butter and oil together in a large frying pan over medium heat, then fry the testicles a handful at a time. (Don't cram them into the frying pan, or they won't fry properly.) When they are lightly browned, remove and place on paper towels to drain any excess fat. Cook the remainder, adding more oil, if needed. Check the seasoning and add more salt and pepper, if desired. Serve with a crisp salad and green bean salad.

PIGS' FEET

If you find jellied pigs' feet for sale, don't turn up your nose; instead, consider yourself very lucky. Snap them up, run home, and invite some adventurous friends over for dinner, because you've found a unique and special food. I'll admit that when I first ate pigs' feet I was confused that there is no meat on them. It takes a trusted friend (that's me, since I've eaten more than my fair share of these beauties) to explain that what you're eating is the slow-cooked, tender skin and the gelatinous parts of the foot, all of which are full of unctuous goodness and deep flavor. It's a love-it-or-hate-it experience, but anyone who enjoys offal—or who hates to waste food—will revel in eating pigs' feet.

It's very easy to find cooked pigs' feet in France, Spain, and Italy, although unfortunately less so in Britain or the United States. They take a long time to cook from scratch (several hours of slow boiling), but, luckily, they also come precooked, set in their own gelatine created by the cooking process. If they haven't already been halved lengthwise, ask the butcher to do this for you, then just heat them up with some toppings before eating with lots of crusty bread.

SERVES 6

3 cooked pigs' feet, halved lengthwise
2 garlic cloves, crushed
a handful of parsley leaves, finely chopped
⅓ cup butter
2 handfuls of bread crumbs
salt and freshly ground black pepper

Remove the feet from the fridge 20 minutes before cooking. Preheat the oven to 400°F. Lay the feet cut-side up in a roasting pan; scatter the garlic and half the parsley on top. Cut thin slivers of butter and lay on top, then sprinkle with bread crumbs, salt, and pepper. Roast uncovered for 20 minutes, then top with the remaining parsley. Serve with gherkins, mustard, lots of crusty French bread, and butter.

INTERACTIVE MEALS

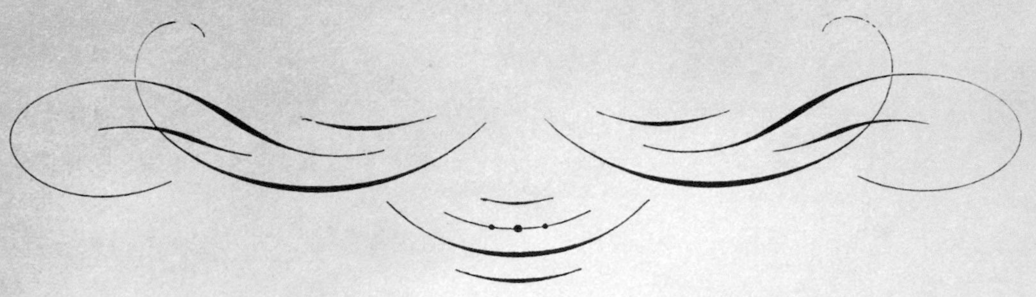

Welcome to my world. I love these interactive meals because my family and friends know that whenever I serve them, supper is bound to turn into a party, and when my family and friends are *that* happy (and *that* noisy) I get a rush of exhilaration and I know that everything is right with the world. It may seem odd to talk about interacting with food, seeing as we all interact with our food by putting it into our mouths, but this chapter is really about the communal act of cooking, where everyone lends a hand. Most of these dishes go just that one step further by getting everyone involved with the raw ingredients themselves, in order to cook their own meals. Oh, and if any single recipe defines this book, it's probably Shabu-shabu, with its hands-on, do-it-yourself, tabletop, free-for-all mayhem. None of the ingredients in it is particularly unusual; it's all in the delivery. If you only make one meal from this book, make Shabu-shabu. You and your friends will neither regret it nor forget it.

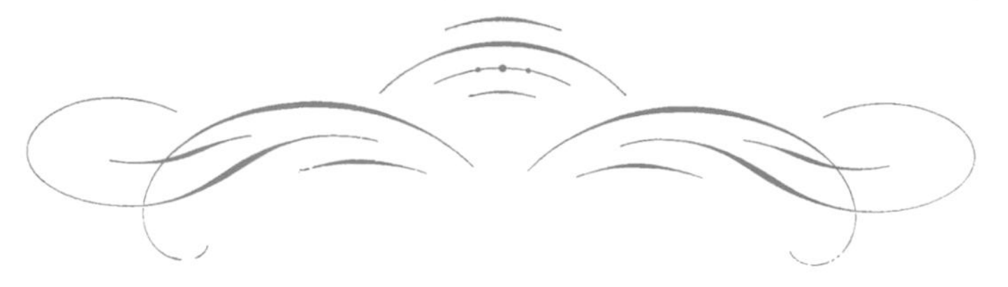

THE LEGENDARY BUM SANDWICH

There's no bum in a bum sandwich. Rather, there's a bum *on* a bum sandwich. You make a sandwich with a set of ingredients that are going to benefit from a little warming and mixing—the original version of this was made with all the ingredients for pesto, for example—and then you wrap it up and sit on it for as long as you can—at least 10 minutes. Your natural heat warms the sandwich up toward body temperature (that's 98.6°F, for anyone who wasn't paying attention in school). Flavor molecules are more active the warmer they are, so a warm sandwich will taste better than a cold one. In addition, your weight squishes the ingredients together, which helps to squeeze the flavor compounds out of the herbs. And it goes without saying that kids love sitting on their sandwiches!

Why is it legendary? Well, when my first book, *Gastronaut*, was published, no one knew me or really understood the crazy ideas in the book, so I needed a good hook to get people talking about it. I came up with the idea of sending a ready-to-sit-on bum sandwich to all the big radio shows, together with a copy of the book. I managed to get host Jonathan Ross to sit on one live on BBC Radio 2 one Saturday morning, and the book got an enormous plug. It worked really well, especially since I recommended that they sit on the sandwich for a whole hour, so they just kept on talking about it! (I've now made bum sandwiches on so many TV shows and live events that I've had to put a stop to it for fear of overdoing it—I now turn down all sandwich-bumming media invitations.)

CREAM CHEESE, THYME, ARUGULA, AND LEMON SANDWICH

MAKES 1 SANDWICH

butter, for spreading
2 slices of bread
cream cheese—enough for 1 sandwich
1 teaspoon fresh thyme leaves
a small handful of arugula salad leaves
olive oil
salt and freshly ground black pepper
½ lemon, zested and reserved

Butter your bread, then spread the cream cheese on one slice and top with the thyme leaves, arugula, and a drizzle of olive oil. Season with salt and pepper, then zest the lemon and scatter it over the top. Add a squeeze of lemon juice and top the sandwich with the other slice of bread.

Wrap the sandwich in several layers of plastic wrap—at least four layers, since you don't want it to split or you'll end up with an oily backside. Now, sit on the sandwich for at least 10 minutes, preferably 20, before unwrapping the warmed sandwich and eating it. Wriggling often helps.

Adventurer

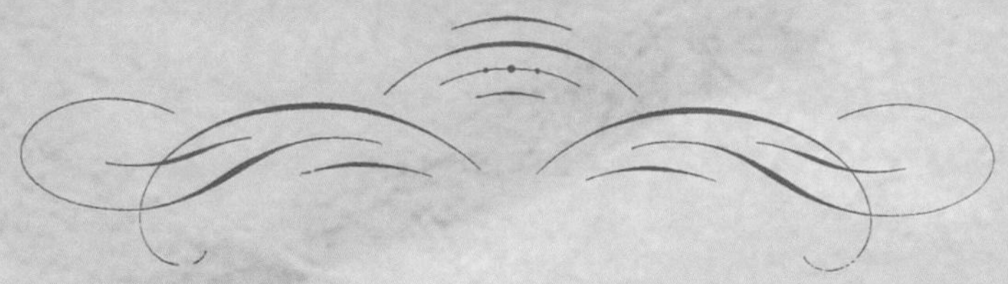

HOW TO FRY AN EGG ON A PIECE OF PAPER

This is one of those "you won't believe it until you see it" recipes, like boiling water in a plastic bottle on a bonfire. It's also potentially dangerous, so children should try this only when supervised by an adult, and, as with flambéing, you should make sure you have a fire extinguisher (or, less dramatically, a sink filled with water) on hand for dousing any unexpected flames.

In essence, this works because the heat from the flame is conducted through the oiled paper, which doesn't burst into flames because it's cooled by the egg. As the egg heats up, the water that it contains heats to 212°F then turns to steam, so the egg remains no hotter than 212°F, which isn't hot enough to burn the paper. Eventually, all the water in the egg will evaporate, but by then it would be overcooked anyway.

The trick is to keep the flame under the parts of the paper that are covered by egg, otherwise there'll be nothing to conduct the heat to, and the paper will absorb all of the heat and be set on fire. You will find it easiest to control if you have a small flame and a tight paper frying pan and you keep moving the pan a little to spread the heat.

YOU WILL NEED

a wire coat hanger
pliers
a clean sheet of letter-size paper (white copy paper is fine)
scissors
8 paper clips
splash of vegetable oil
pastry brush
1 egg
the smallest gas burner on your stove (or a gas camp stove)
bowl of water (or fire extinguisher) for disaster prevention

First, make your coat hanger saucepan: Grip the top of the coat hanger with one hand, and the middle of the long straight bottom edge with the other and pull until the coat hanger is turned into a long thin square.

Using pliers, twist the wire at the bottom corner of the coat hanger until you have a second handle. Place the wire square on a table and press it into shape until it sits flat.

Cut the sheet of white paper so that it is ½–1in larger than the wire shape on each side. Place the wire square on top of the paper, then fold the edges of the paper over the wire and secure with paper clips. You now have your paper "frying pan." Again, check that it sits flat on a table to make sure that the egg won't slip off.

Place a bowl of water or fire extinguisher nearby in case of flames. Brush a little oil all over the paper. Place the "frying pan" onto a flat surface, folded edges pointing upward, and crack the egg into the middle of it.

Turn on a small, controllable flame. Carefully pick up the pan and hold it over the flame—it shouldn't be too close. Gently move it around so that the heat is spread under the whole egg, but make sure that you heat only the paper that's covered by the egg—and don't be impatient! If you see the paper start to smoke, lift the "pan" a little higher. After about 1–2 minutes you should see the egg white starting to turn opaque, and after another 5 minutes or so the whole egg should be cooked. Eat it right off the paper.

CREPES

Crepes must be the simplest and most reliable crowd-pleasers in the food world; whenever we make them at home we have a whale of a time, regardless of whether or not anyone's attempt ends in success or disaster. Just because the odd-off crepe is a mess doesn't make it inedible, and if you really do destroy one, or plaster it to the ceiling, you can always make another—it's just flour, milk, and eggs, after all. The one rule in our house is that you *have* to flip. None of that putting a plate over the top and turning the crepe to keep it perfect. But, fear not—we will applaud the disasters as loudly as the successes, and better to have flipped and flopped than never to have flipped at all. So I implore you not to save crepes for Mardi Gras every year, but, instead, to whip them up with your friends for a cheap, fun supper or breakfast whenever the mood strikes you.

This is the ridiculously simple recipe for good, old-fashioned crepes that I've eaten since I was a kid. The classic way to eat them is with sugar and a squeeze of lemon, but I still love golden syrup (as do my kids) and maple syrup is great, too, or you can make savory crepes—goat cheese with some ham or a scattering of thyme leaves is delicious. Of course, you can wrap pretty much anything in them.

MAKES 12 CREPES
2 cups all-purpose flour
2 medium free-range eggs
3 cups whole milk
¾ cup butter, for frying

TO SERVE
a selection of golden syrup, maple syrup, sugar, lemon, ham, soft cheeses, watercress, arugula salad, herbs…

Sift the flour into a mixing bowl, add the eggs, and whisk them in with a fork. Slowly add in the milk, splash by splash, whisking as you go, until you have a smooth batter. Some people like to rest the batter for 30 minutes, but you don't really need to.

Put a medium-sized frying pan (ideally, one that has gently sloped sides for good flipping action) over medium heat and add a pat of butter. When it's bubbling and beginning to brown, add a ladleful of batter and tip the frying pan around so that the batter coats the base of the frying pan. Cook it for 2–3 minutes, until you can see the edges crisping up, then flip it over. (If you don't have a reliable method, try the "J" method, where you drop the frying pan down, then flip it back up again while pulling it toward you to send the crepe off the edge of the pan and curving through the air. Take a look at www.gastronaut.com for a little instructional video.) Cook for another minute or so on the other side, then slide the crepe onto a plate and serve with a selection of fillings.

Add another pat of butter and then more batter for the next crepe. Try not to let the butter blacken (carefully wipe the pan with paper towels if it does). Oh, and make sure that everyone gets a turn!

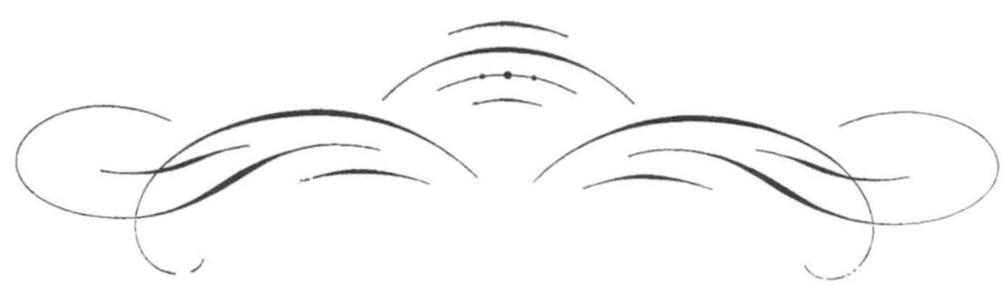

SAVORY DO-IT-YOURSELF TARTS

This is the perfect solution for the times when you've invited a friend for dinner who happens to be a brilliant cook, or—heaven forbid—a celebrity chef. Instead of jumping through hoops trying to think of something ridiculously extravagant to match their expectations, get them to do the work!

What you do is place all the ingredients on the table, including a chunk of puff pastry, then hand around one greased baking sheet between each pair of guests and let them make their own tarts. They do all the hard work, indulging their gustatory preferences and creating a little work of wonder; all you have to do is slip the tarts in the oven for 15 minutes, then deliver the finished product back to them. Make-your-own pizza is a variation on this theme, but do-it-yourself tarts are even easier, because it's pretty much impossible to mess up a puff pastry tart.

(You can, of course, do dessert in the same way: see Sweet Do-It-Yourself Tarts, page 192.)

SERVES 6

16oz package of puff pastry
flour, for dusting
butter, for greasing
olive oil
salt and freshly ground black pepper
arugula salad, to serve

FOR THE TOPPINGS (AS WITH PIZZAS, YOU WON'T NEED MUCH OF EACH)
goat cheese, cut or ripped into chunks
fresh rosemary, thyme, and basil
red peppers, sliced
asparagus, blanched
mushrooms, sliced and tossed in a little olive oil
peas, fava beans, or spinach
very sweet tomatoes
slices of salami, chorizo, or cured ham
sweet chiles

Preheat the oven to 400°F. On a floured surface, roll the pastry out to the thickness of about ⅛in and then cut into 6 large slices or 12 small ones in whatever shapes you like. Lightly grease two or three baking sheets, dust with a little all-purpose flour, and place the pastry pieces on them with a good 1in gap between each. Place the baking sheets on the table, along with the topping ingredients.

Encourage your friends to experiment with the toppings, advising them that delicate ingredients like ham, basil, and spinach should be at the bottom of the layering or they will dry out. Season the finished tarts, then take the baking sheets away and bake uncovered for 15–18 minutes, until crusty and golden around the edges.

Drizzle a little olive oil over the tarts and return them to your friends piping hot. Serve with some arugula salad.

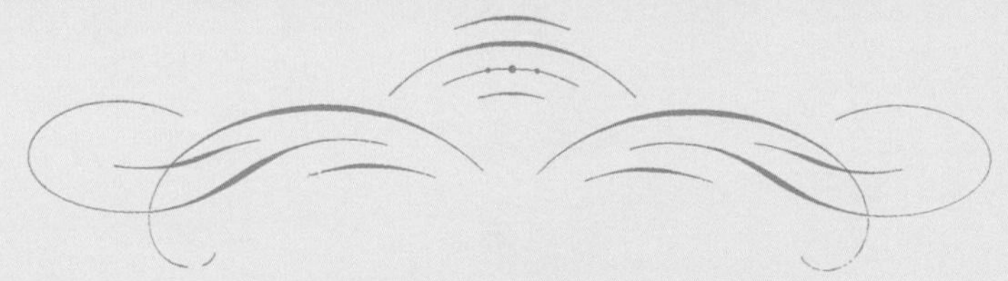

SALMON TARTARE WITH CUCUMBER AND GREEN BEAN SALAD

One of the great things about steak tartare is the do-it-yourself aspect—being given all the flavoring ingredients so you can essentially build a meal yourself—and the same is true with salmon tartare.

Salmon tartare is much less daunting to make at home than steak tartare—it ranges from exquisitely delicate to punchy and herby, depending on how you throw yours together. The fun lies in putting all the ingredients on the table ready for your friends to dig into as they wish.

HINT: If you have a circular table you can just put everything in the middle, with a plate in front of each of your friends, and let them get to it. However, if your table is rectangular (like mine is), you really need to split the ingredients into several bowls so they are in easy reach for everyone.

SERVES 6

1¾lb very fresh salmon fillet, skinned and boned
1 teaspoon superfine sugar
½ teaspoon salt

FOR THE SALAD
1lb green beans
1 whole cucumber, peeled
a handful of fresh dill, chopped
2 tablespoons olive oil
2 teaspoons white wine vinegar (or sherry vinegar)
salt and freshly ground black pepper

TO SERVE
sourdough toast and butter
1 tablespoon finely chopped shallots
a large handful of parsley leaves, finely chopped
2 lemons, each cut into 6 segments
2 tablespoons capers, finely chopped
2 tablespoons gherkins, finely chopped
Tabasco sauce
Worcestershire sauce

Using a sharp knife, chop the salmon into small pieces about the size of coffee beans (don't use a food processor, since this will create a paste—you want to maintain the texture of the fish). Put the salmon pieces in a bowl, sprinkle with the sugar and salt, and combine thoroughly. Cover and refrigerate for 30 minutes (which is just about the same amount of time it takes to do all of the following).

To make the salad, boil or steam the green beans until just tender, then rinse in plenty of cold water (they need to be cool, but this also keeps them vividly green). Shave the whole cucumber into very thin slivers using a vegetable peeler or mandolin. Put the beans and cucumber into a large bowl. Combine the dill, olive oil, vinegar, a pinch of salt, and a few grinds of black pepper in a bowl and mix thoroughly. Pour this over the cucumbers and beans and toss well.

Toast slices of sourdough bread on a ridged grill pan or in a toaster. Put the shallots, parsley, lemon segments, capers, and gherkins into separate small bowls.

Give each person a plate or bowl and a spoon for serving. Put the salmon, salads, and toasts on the table in large bowls and place all the other ingredients on the table around them. Everyone builds a personal bowl of tartare to suit their taste (just as with beef tartare), starting with a small mound of salmon. The flavorings should be mixed into the salmon to each individual's liking. Start with a squeeze of lemon and add the other flavorings as you see fit.

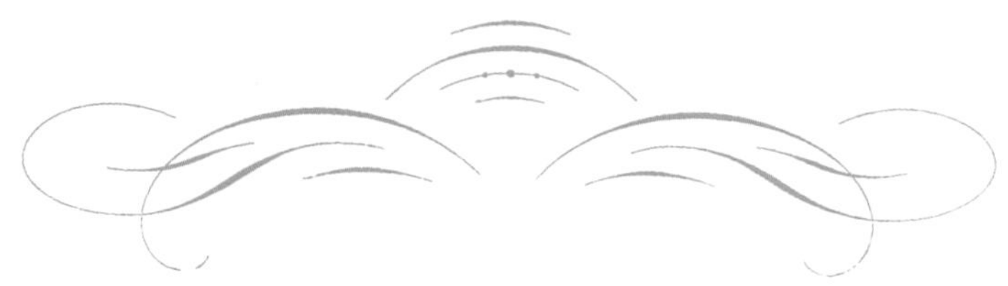

SHRIMP IN LIME, GINGER, CILANTRO, AND GARLIC

This is one of my family's favorite meals of all time. It's terrifically easy to make, but the heavenly combination of flavors and the sheer exhilaration of eating hot, fragrant buttery shrimp with sticky fingers, and then soaking bread into the remaining juices, seems to inspire and enliven everyone. I don't care what Darwin said: *this* is why opposable thumbs were invented.

A big part of the experience is the informal, messy method of eating. You really need to get hands-on with the food to enjoy it, so I urge you not to offer your friends any cutlery, since that will destroy the sensual experience. Just give them a few paper napkins. Once you've cooked the shrimp, simply put the pan in the middle of the table, alongside lots of crusty bread, squeeze the juice of a lime over the top, and have everyone dig in.

SERVES 6

¾ cup butter (use less if you're worried about your cholesterol, more if you're feeling decadent)
10 garlic cloves, peeled and crushed
1 large thumb of ginger, grated
3 ½lb fresh-cooked coldwater shrimp
1 bunch of cilantro, stems finely chopped and leaves roughly chopped
zest and juice of 2 limes
salt and freshly ground black pepper
crusty bread, to serve

Take a large, wide, heavy-bottomed saucepan or frying pan with a lid. Put it on low heat and add the butter and garlic. Fry very gently for 5 minutes, then stir in the ginger, shrimp, and cilantro stems (reserving the leaves).

Put the lid on the pan and cook for about 10–20 minutes (depending on how cold your shrimp were when they went in), stirring gently but frequently to mix all the flavors together. Check that the shrimp are piping hot, but don't cook them (they were cooked already, so they really just need to be warmed through).

When they are ready, add the cilantro leaves, stir thoroughly, and place the pan on the table. Scatter the lime zest on top, squeeze the lemon juice over the shrimp, and add plenty of salt and freshly ground black pepper. Serve with crusty bread, and dig in.

VEGETABLE INSTRUMENTS

Yup, with a little whittling, you can make a carrot into a flute, a pumpkin into a bongo, and a butternut squash into an unholy sounding, crazy-assed bassoon! It may sound like a ridiculous use of fresh vegetables, but it does have a long and noble history—the Indian snake-charmer's *pungi* is made from the bottle gourd, the Japanese *tonkori* has strings of vegetable fibers (although it does make a *horrible* sound), and the Votic bagpipe *rakkopilli* was made of a pig's bladder. People have been making sweet harmony from their lunch for thousands of years, and there's even a modern orchestra that plays exclusively on vegetables—the Viennese Vegetable Orchestra—and they are quite good!

There are lots of different ways you can tease simple tunes out of fruits and vegetables, but the sweeter and more controllable the sound, the more complex the design. I'm going to talk you through some basic instruments to get you started. The flow of air in these things can be complex and variable, so you have to be prepared to sacrifice the occasional one to the soup pot without getting so much as a squeak out of it. Plan to make several for sharing anyway. Sometimes it's just whittler's luck.

A note on storage: To stop your completed instruments from turning brown and limp, keep them in a bowl of water in the fridge.

When you've finished using your vegetables for making beautiful music, don't throw them away; they can still make a wonderful soup as long as you boil them thoroughly to sterilize them!

VERDI
REQUIEM
RICORDI

BUTTERNUT SQUASH PUNGI/BASSOON

This one is incredibly easy to make. You need a long butternut squash (for some reason, the longer ones produce a better range of notes) or a huge daikon radish. You'll also need some straws for mouthpieces (they work like the double reed on an oboe or bassoon), an electric drill, a medium-sized drill bit the same width as your straws (usually ¼in), and an extra-long wide drill bit for hollowing out the squash.

If you are using a squash, cut off 2in from the thick end at the bottom—you need to cut off enough to expose the chamber holding the seeds. Then scoop out the seeds.

Drill a small hole from the top (the thin end) toward the thicker end, going as far as you can with the drill bit. Then turn the squash over, change to the large drill bit, and drill a larger chamber from the thicker end of the squash or daikon radish up to meet the thinner hole. Check that the hole goes all the way through and that it's clear of vegetable debris.

Cut the straw in half and then chop one end into a sharp arrow shape. Push the other end into the squash or daikon radish and blow. Again, it takes a little experimentation to find the pitch, playing with the depth of the straw and the force of blow, but you should be able to replicate the sound of a snake-charmer's pungi.

PUMPKIN OR CELERY ROOT BONGOS

This is even easier. You need two or three good, very solid fruits for this, and they should be of different sizes to produce different notes. Cut a 1in-diameter hole from the base end and then use a teaspoon and small sharp knife to remove the stringy innards, without destroying the structural integrity of the vegetable—it should be sturdy, but hollow. Experiment with playing it, covering the opening a little with one hand as you pat the bongo with carrots, hands, or wooden spoons.

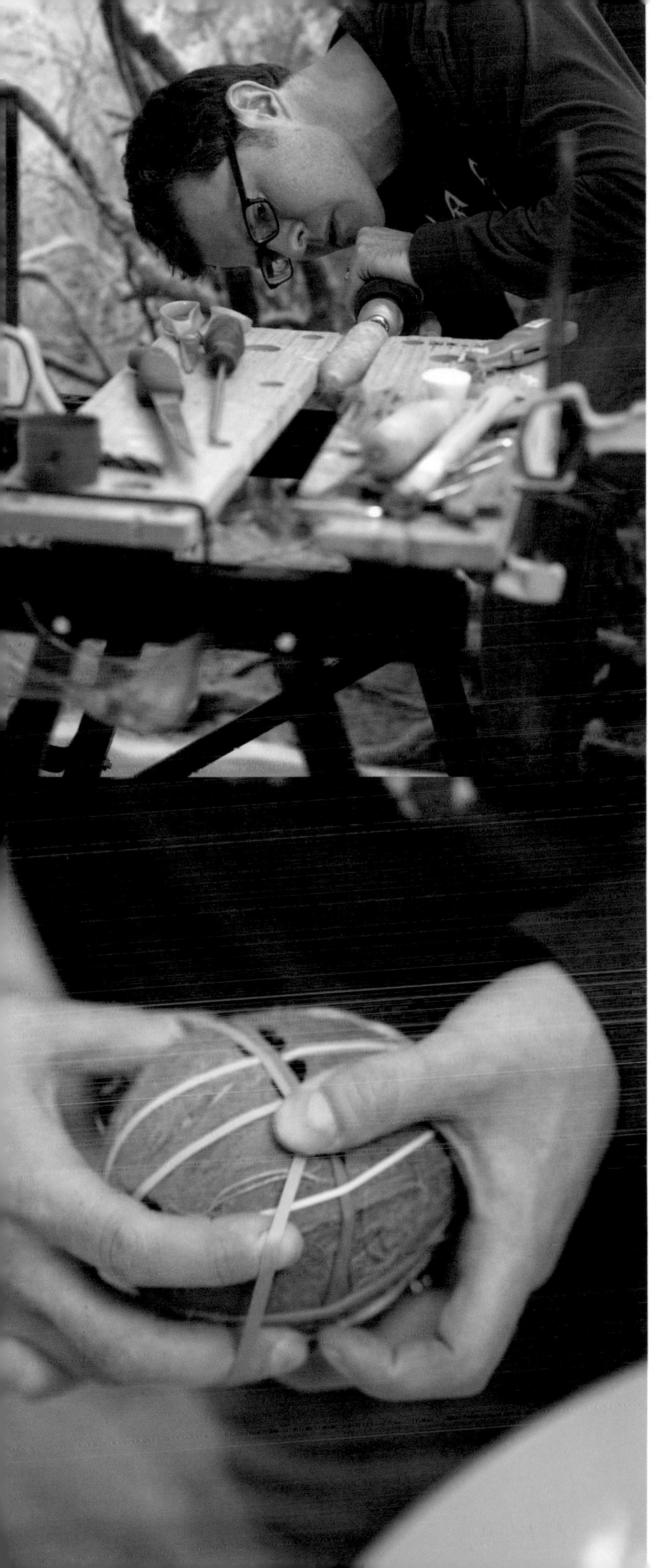

CARROT FLUTES

This is an end-blown flute—a sort of cross between a flute and a whistle. You hold it with the carrot pointing directly away from you, but the sound comes by blowing *over* a hole, rather than into it.

You'll need some large carrots, a small sharp knife, and a drill with various drill bits, including a very long one.

First, cut a short slice off each end to flatten the carrot for drilling. Next, drill a wide (½in) hole all the way through your carrot. The easiest way is to start with a small drill bit and then change it for a long, thick one. If your drill bit is shorter than the carrot, you'll have to do one end first, then continue from the other end. Be careful, please, and operate the drill only at low speed.

Now, drill three finger-holes somewhere near the middle of the carrot using a ¼in drill bit. To tell the truth, the finger holes are a bit hit-and-miss, and their effectiveness depends on the aerodynamics within your particular carrot. You'll probably find that covering some of the air holes changes the pitch, but covering others makes no difference.

Now, create the all-important mouthpiece. The most effective design I've used involves shaving a short section off the back edge to allow your lips to get behind the blowhole, then shaving a longer one off the front edge, cutting slightly into the circular through-hole to create the mouthpiece that you will blow over.

Experiment with various angles and different strengths of blowing. It may seem as though your flute isn't working, and then you'll suddenly get the hang of it. Often, a gentle toot will make it sing!

COCONUT RATTLE

This one's obvious, really. Simply cut open the coconut as carefully as you can and scoop out the flesh. Then fill it with dried beans and cover with rubber bands to hold your instrument together.

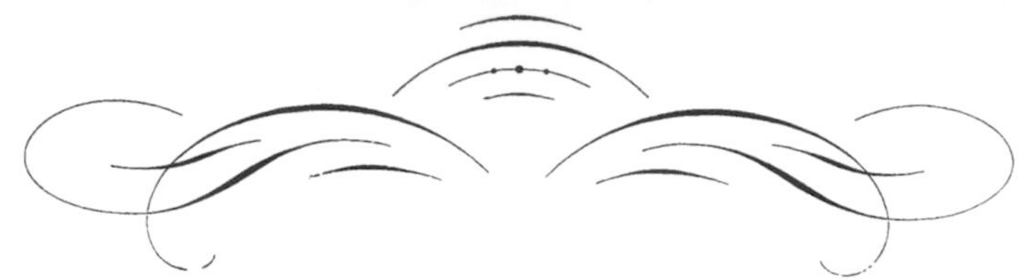

SKEWERS COOKED ON A CAR ENGINE

It's possibly the most ridiculous recipe in this book, if not in the world, but it does work; I've tried it—and on national TV, too. The inspiration came from a book called *Manifold Destiny: The One! The Only! Guide to Cooking on Your Car Engine* by Chris Maynard and Bill Scheller.

But let's just ease off the gas a minute. All cars are different, and much as I dislike them, they are both useful and inordinately expensive, so unless you're sure of your car's sweet skewer spot, the next time you take your car in to be serviced be sure to ask where you could strap a skewer to a very hot part of the engine without damaging anything. You'll find your mechanic is so intrigued and excited at the prospect of you doing something so wild that he will indulge your ridiculous question. (If you need a hint, it's often a good idea to strap your skewer to the manifold.)

All you need to do is build a little wire cage that doesn't interfere with any of the workings of the engine, then wrap a skewer's-worth of fish and soft vegetables (e.g., zucchinis) in foil and strap them on. The next time you have a road trip coming up, try it; you should have a gently cooked parcel of food ready to eat when you arrive. But please don't travel 50 miles just to cook a skewer. That would be silly.

MAKES 2 SKEWERS

9oz salmon or white fish of your choosing, cut into 1in cubes
¼lb zucchini, cut into 1in cubes
¼lb red peppers, cut into 1in cubes
1 tablespoon extra-virgin olive oil
1 tablespoon soy sauce or ponzu (citrus seasoned soy sauce)—it's in the photo!
1 teaspoon fresh thyme leaves
1 teaspoon fresh rosemary leaves
salt and freshly ground black pepper

Take two large skewers and spike the fish and vegetables onto them, alternating the vegetable and fish chunks. Lay the skewers on a bed of foil, splash each with the olive oil and soy sauce or ponzu, and scatter the herbs and seasoning over the top. Wrap up really tightly in the foil, then wrap again in several more layers, using one continuous piece of foil to make sure that no fumes from the engine can make their way in. However, you need to strike a balance: too much foil and the skewers won't cook; too little and engine fumes could contaminate them.

Using some strong, unpainted wire or chicken-wire, make a rudimentary cage to fit your foil-wrapped skewers, place them inside it and hook it firmly around the part of the engine approved by your mechanic using some more wire. All engines are different, but the shortest cooking trip I've ever done was a drive of 40 minutes, covering about 25 miles, on a nice summer's day and the skewer was just cooked. An hour is probably most reliable, and if it's not nice and warm, I'd plan to go a bit farther. When you arrive at your destination, carefully remove the skewer and check to see that it's hot and cooked all the way through. Then check that it doesn't smell of car fumes. If all is well, tuck in!

Mitsukan
味ぽん
AJIPON
GREAT ON

BANANA LEAF TAKEOUT FEAST

Oh, the sheer nerve of it. Yes, this recipe really does include one entire takeout meal for six. If you have friends coming over for dinner but you're not going to get home until five minutes before they're due to arrive, this is an excellent way to rescue an evening. If your friends are like mine, they don't mind what they eat, as long as it's served with love. So buy a bundle of banana leaves from a specialty Indian, Chinese, or Thai supermarket and keep it in the fridge (it will last for a couple of weeks). On the day of your meal, order a takeout meal from your favorite Indian restaurant to be delivered when you get home.

When I serve this for my friends, we all eat using our fingers, and I really urge you to try it, too. It's an extraordinary sensation and it makes a meal into a sensual extravaganza—I just can't recommend it enough. I have a wonderful Keralan Indian restaurant nearby and its food is sweet, fragrant, and sublimely coconutty, perfect for this leaf-based meal. When you've finished, the leaves and scraps all go into the compost bin, so there are no dishes to do either. Of course, there's no point in fibbing about the source of your food—its origin is all part of the fun!

A little while ago I made a TV series all about feasts around the world, and in Kerala I took part in the extraordinary Sadya feast as part of the Onam celebrations, which welcome the mythical King Mahabali back home for his annual visit. For the feast, almost 30 million people across the state sit down to exactly the same meal at exactly the same time, regardless of their faith, wealth, or social status. It's a remarkable and typically Keralan display of solidarity, and every meal is eaten on a banana leaf.

SERVES 6

6 large banana leaves
a takeout Indian meal for 6

This is traditionally eaten with everyone sitting on the floor, using their fingers. I wouldn't worry too much about the floor, but you really should try eating with your fingers.

Order around nine different dishes, wipe your banana leaves with a damp cloth before use, then put a little of each dish around the edge of each banana leaf, with a big pile of rice in the middle.

At the end of your meal, just fold up the banana leaves and throw everything in the compost bin.

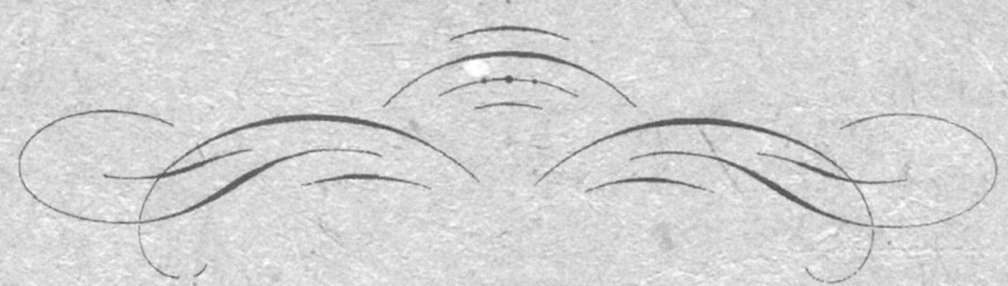

CRAB AND HAMMER PARTY

The unfettered pleasure of walloping a crab with a hammer—hang the consequences—is what a crab-and-hammer party is all about. Maybe it's just me, but sometimes there's this exhilarating urge to throw caution and manners to the wind, grab the kitchen table, hoik it into the backyard, and make a huge mess of lunch. There are few better ways of having fun with your food and your friends, and this is without question my favorite way to eat—the very definition of an extraordinary meal.

Often, the most spectacular feasts are the simplest, and this one is ridiculously easy. If you wanted to, you could catch the crabs yourself and boil them in a huge pot of salted water (we've done this before and it's wonderful), but no one would hold it against you if you decided to buy some lovely, freshly cooked crabs (and maybe a lobster, too, if you're feeling flush) from the fish market. (Buy them the same day you eat them.) I'd urge you to make your own mayonnaise, though—it's delicious and pretty easy.

If you own enough hammers for all of your guests, you are either a construction worker or a bit weird. Ask your friends to bring their own hammers and perhaps some goggles (these aren't really needed, but do add to the fun!) and maybe a shirt or apron that they don't mind getting messy. Give each one a crab, a fork, and a cutting board (if you care for your table) and let the mayhem commence. You can, of course, do all of this in the comfort of your own kitchen/dining room/studio apartment—but no food fights!

One medium-sized cooked crab per person (1¾–2¼lb each—if larger, serve one crab between two people; male crabs are best)
plenty of mayonnaise (see page 121)
lemon wedges
crusty bread and butter and some fine ales, to serve

If you've bought live crabs, drop them in boiling water, bring back to a boil, and cook for 12 minutes (up to 2¼lb) or 18 minutes (up to 4½lb), then remove and leave to cool.

If you've bought cooked crabs, keep them in the fridge until near crabfest time. Clean your table and set it with all the food and tools (and a cutting board, if your table is posh). Give each person a little bowl of mayo, a wedge of lemon, and a crab, and let rip.

MAYONNAISE

A LITTLE GUIDE TO DISMANTLING A CRAB

If you need advice about how to dismantle your crab, here are the basics. Start by pulling all the legs and claws off for individual meat-mining, then pull the entire underbody away from the main shell by placing the crab upended, eyes down on a board, and pushing against the leg casing until the body detaches. Discard the dead men's fingers you find inside (you'll know them when you spot them) and any stringy gills and plasticky-looking pieces. Cut each of the main body-casings in half with a large strong knife to allow access to the nuggets of flesh inside, and then get cracking, hammering, picking, sucking, and pulling, not forgetting the utterly delicious brown meat inside the main shell.

Georgia swears by making mayonnaise by hand, to the extent that I feel tangibly guilty when she catches me making it in a food processor. She's right, too; you can taste a little sprinkling of love in handmade mayo. It really doesn't take that much longer, either—probably as long as it takes to wash a food processor. Keep spare mayo in the fridge—it will last for at least 2 days.

MAKES 2 CUPS

2 large egg yolks
1 teaspoon Dijon or English mustard
salt and freshly ground black pepper
1 cup sunflower oil
⅓ cup non-virgin olive oil
zest and juice of ½ lemon
finely chopped cilantro or thyme
    (optional)

HANDMADE METHOD

Put a damp cloth down and place a large mixing bowl on top (the cloth will stop the bowl from skidding around). Add the egg yolks, mustard, salt, and pepper to the bowl and mix together using a whisk or wooden spoon. Add the two oils in a slow drizzle, stirring all the time and making sure that everything mixes to a firm, fluffy mayo. When you have used up all the oil, slowly add the lemon zest and juice, continuing to whisk. Check for seasoning, and if you are adding herbs fold them in now. Stand back and feel proud.

FOOD-PROCESSOR METHOD (SORRY, GEORGIA)

Put the egg yolks in the food processor and add the mustard and a good pinch of salt and a grind of pepper. Blend to mix them together, then, with the food processor still running, carefully add the sunflower and olive oils in a slow trickle. The mixture should stay nice and thick and have a good yellow color. Next, gradually add the lemon zest and juice. The mayonnaise will loosen a little and turn slightly paler in color. Check for seasoning and if you are adding herbs fold them in now.

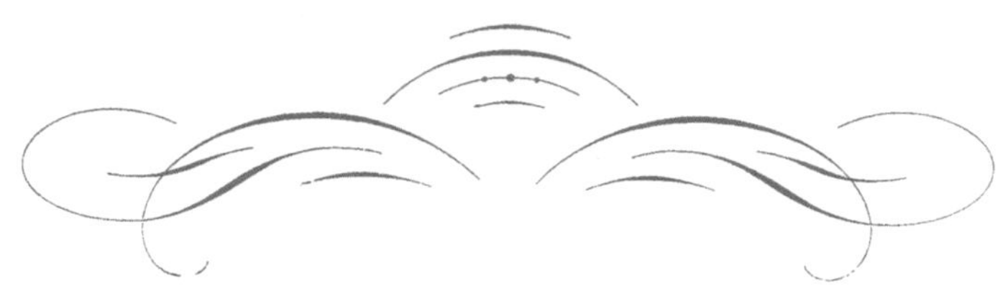

SUSHI ROLLING PARTY

Sushi-making is *fantastic*, and my friends all have a wild time whenever we make this, intoxicated by the sheer culinary mayhem. I know that some people think sushi is complicated, while others are scared of serving raw fish. However, I implore you to try this out with your friends; you'll have a riot making it and you'll discover a whole culinary world that's fascinating, healthy (just use very fresh fish), and cheap, to boot. If you find it tricky making sushi for the first time, that's absolutely fine—learning alongside your friends is fun, and transforms terrible technique into glorious failure.

It's easy to throw a sushi party. All the ingredients and equipment you need are available in big supermarkets these days, including seaweed sheets and bamboo sushi-rolling mats (these are pretty cheap, so buy a few—one mat shared between two guests is perfect). If you can't find wasabi, English mustard or (even better) freshly grated horseradish are great substitutes.

So, what preparation is needed? Well, you need to cook the sushi rice and prepare the fillings beforehand, taking good care of your salmon (see note on page 149 about freezing salmon), although you can have the fish prepared for you at the fish counter. If it's your first time, I wouldn't complicate things; stick to sushi rolls using salmon, cucumber, and avocado. I often put a few plates of sashimi (raw fish) around the table, too (see page 147), and you'll see from the photo that strips of mackerel are also great to use. You might be surprised to find that most fish is fantastic to eat raw—my favorites are salmon, mackerel, red snapper, sea bass, and butterfish.

Bear in mind that one person will need to cut the long sushi rolls into the smaller mouth-sized portions on a cutting board (I tend to do this for everyone). Make sure your very sharp knife is wiped clean after cutting each roll—otherwise, the starch left on the knife makes it a bit sticky and clumsy to use. If you're doing this for lots of people, the cutting can keep you busy, but it adds to the mayhem and fun.

The recipe here is the pared-down, entry-level approach to sushi—once you've tried this, you'll probably want to spread your wings, refine your technique, and explore the wonderful world of kombu, ponzu, and katsuobushi.

SERVES 6

3 cups sushi rice
½ cup rice vinegar
⅓ cup superfine sugar (or mirin)
3 teaspoons salt
(the above 3 ingredients can be substituted for ¾ cup preseasoned sushi rice vinegar, if you've bought it)

1⅓ lb very fresh wild salmon fillet, skinned and boned (or 14oz salmon and 3 mackerel fillets prepared as for Sashimi, see page 148)
1 red pepper
2 cucumbers
2 ripe avocados
20 nori seaweed sheets
wasabi powder (or English mustard or freshly grated horseradish)
light soy sauce, for dipping

TO SERVE (OPTIONAL)
sake, pickled ginger, and a selection of Japanese or Chinese pickled vegetables

キッコーマン

First, cook your rice, since it will need time to cool a little before eating. Place it in a strainer, rinse with cold water until the water runs clear, then transfer to a large saucepan with 3 cups cold water. Bring to a boil, stir, and turn the heat down. Keep it boiling for 5 minutes, with the lid on (making sure it doesn't boil over), then reduce the heat and simmer for another 10 minutes, stirring so that it doesn't stick and burn. Turn off the heat and leave the rice in the covered pan for another 10 minutes. It should be lightly sticky but not soggy.

Meanwhile, mix together the rice seasonings—the vinegar, superfine sugar, and salt—and stir until the sugar has dissolved. Add the mixture to the cooked rice and gently stir through so the rice is shiny and sticky. Spoon it into a wide bowl, then leave to cool for at least 30 minutes—it's best served at room temperature (if you can wait that long). Once it's at room temperature, you can cover the bowl with a dish towel. The rice can be served on the table in two or three separate bowls for easy access.

Now, on to your salmon (see note on page 149 about freezing salmon). Make sure all the bones were removed at the fish counter (if not, pull them out using a clean pair of tweezers or pliers), then cut the fillet into long, thin pencil-sized pieces and arrange them on two plates for serving. If you're adding some extra sashimi (see page 146) to the mix, prepare these now.

Deseed the pepper and cucumber and cut into pencil-thin strips. Peel the avocado and cut it, too, into pencil-thin slices. Put all the vegetables into bowls.

Tip: If you're making rice for more than 10 people it may be best to make it in two batches, so that it is easier to handle. It takes a long time for a big pan of rice to come to a boil, and it can turn into a soggy mess.

SERVING

Put the rolling mats and all the ingredients around the table ready for sushi-making, along with napkins and some shared finger bowls for wetting hands (these are very important!) Each person will need a small side plate and a little bowl or cup for soy sauce. You'll also need one sharp knife, a damp cloth to keep it clean, and a cutting board ready to cut the rolls into portions.

Photocopy the next page, cut out the instructions, and give a copy to each of your friends. Have fun!

A NOTE ABOUT SOY SAUCE

Not all soy sauces are created equal, not by a long shot. Don't, whatever you do, use heavy or strong Chinese soy sauce—that way lies sushi madness. Do your best to get your hands on Kikkoman's Sashimi Shoyu (it's just another word for soy, but this stuff is sublime). It's a little more expensive than run-of-the-mill soy sauce, but it really is worth the extra cash. It's a gentle and perfectly balanced blend of soy and wheat, brewed for much higher levels of umami (the fifth taste in the mouth, which can be roughly translated as savory).

HOW TO MAKE SUSHI ROLLS

Hello. Your hosts figure that you are both adventurous and dexterous enough to make your own sushi (and no, they're not just being lazy). Today's task is to make sushi rolls. You aren't expected to be excellent at it the first time—in fact, early attempts are expected to end in glorious failure—but, hopefully, by the end of the meal you'll have cracked it. Good luck!

LONG SUSHI ROLLS (FUTO MAKI)

1. Take a sushi rolling mat and place it in front of you, with the bamboo strips running horizontally (you'll be rolling it away from you). Lay a rectangle of the dark green nori seaweed on top of it, shiny side down and with the long side running horizontally (i.e. panorama, not portrait).

2. Wet your hands with a little cold water (this is REALLY important), then grab a large handful of sushi rice and spread it across the nearest two-thirds of the seaweed sheet until it is just under ½in thick.

3. Dip your finger into the wasabi and spread a long, thin smear of it horizontally across the middle of the rice.

4. Place one long, thin line of the filling of your choice across the middle of the rice. Not too much, however, or you won't be able to roll it up.

5. Now, lift the edge of the mat nearest you and gently, but firmly, roll the sushi up around the filling, squeezing gently. Press firmly and make sure the edge of the roll sticks down (use a damp finger to wet the edge if you need to help it stick down).

6. Unroll the mat to leave behind the finished roll, and ask someone to use a clean, wet knife to cut it into 1¼–1½in slices. Dip each into a little soy sauce and munch.

Good job! If you made something of a mess of the first one, don't worry—most of us do. Try another, and you'll soon get the hang of it.

HOW TO MAKE SUSHI ROLLS

Hello. Your hosts figure that you are both adventurous and dexterous enough to make your own sushi (and no, they're not just being lazy). Today's task is to make sushi rolls. You aren't expected to be excellent at it the first time—in fact, early attempts are expected to end in glorious failure—but, hopefully, by the end of the meal you'll have cracked it. Good luck!

LONG SUSHI ROLLS (FUTO MAKI)

1. Take a sushi rolling mat and place it in front of you, with the bamboo strips running horizontally (you'll be rolling it away from you). Lay a rectangle of the dark green nori seaweed on top of it, shiny side down and with the long side running horizontally (i.e. panorama, not portrait).

2. Wet your hands with a little cold water (this is REALLY important), then grab a large handful of sushi rice and spread it across the nearest two-thirds of the seaweed sheet until it is just under ½in thick.

3. Dip your finger into the wasabi and spread a long, thin smear of it horizontally across the middle of the rice.

4. Place one long, thin line of the filling of your choice across the middle of the rice. Not too much, however, or you won't be able to roll it up.

5. Now, lift the edge of the mat nearest you and gently, but firmly, roll the sushi up around the filling, squeezing gently. Press firmly and make sure the edge of the roll sticks down (use a damp finger to wet the edge if you need to help it stick down).

6. Unroll the mat to leave behind the finished roll, and ask someone to use a clean, wet knife to cut it into 1¼–1½in slices. Dip each into a little soy sauce and munch.

Good job! If you made something of a mess of the first one, don't worry—most of us do. Try another, and you'll soon get the hang of it.

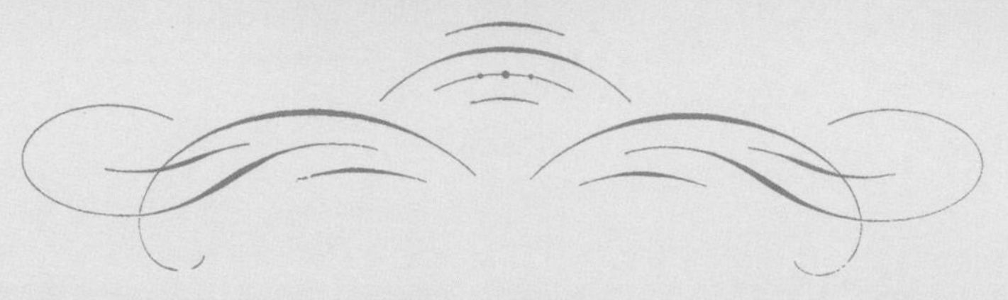

QUAILS MAYHEM

There's a simple, scientific explanation as to why quails taste so good: because they are small, they have a high surface-to-volume ratio. This means, basically, that you get more skin per mouthful of meat, and, as we all know, the skin is where the flavor is. However, unlike chickens, which have a fair bit of fat under the skin (which the weight-conscious among you may be wary of), quail skin is pretty lean, with just enough fat to make it meaty and sweetly crispy, but not so much that it will expand your waistline. There's also something a little extraordinary about having a whole bird to yourself.

I like to serve this with no cutlery on the table, so that my friends get thoroughly finger-lickingly involved with their food. With that in mind, you'll need napkins! The trick is to wait until the birds are cool enough to touch (they need to rest anyway to be at their best), and serve them with just some nice crusty bread, or with other finger-friendly vegetables, such as small carrots and baby new potatoes.

How many quails can one person eat? Some might say that one per person is too few, but if you're eating every last morsel by gnawing the whole thing, two per person would be profligate. I used to swear that serving too much was part of the fun of a feast, but I've changed my ways when it comes to meat. Perhaps serve one per person, and give your friends lots of fantastic bread to go with it.

SERVES 6

6 garlic cloves, finely chopped
¼ cup Dijon mustard
1 tablespoon fresh thyme leaves
3 tablespoons olive oil
salt and freshly ground black pepper
6 quails
plenty of crusty bread, to serve

Bring the garlic, mustard, thyme leaves, olive oil, and seasoning together in a large bowl, and mix to create a messy sauce. Roll the quails in the sauce, rubbing it into the skin using your hands, and push a little of it into the quails' cavities, too. Set aside (not in the fridge) to marinate for a little while (30 minutes would be great, but 10 minutes will do the trick).

Preheat the broiler, lay some foil over your grill pan, and place the quails on it. Broil them for about 5–10 minutes, until nicely browned and crispy, then turn them over and broil the other side for another 5–6 minutes. I like to serve them a little pink in the legs, but do make sure that the juices run clear (free of blood) when pricked at the thigh with a knife. Serve with a big basket of bread.

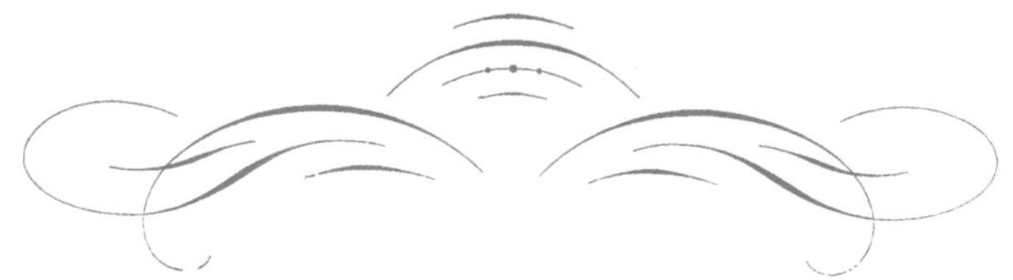

WHOLE CRISPY DUCK WITH CREPES

It's odd that people don't make crispy duck at home more often when it's so popular at Chinese restaurants. Perhaps it sounds unapproachably difficult to make or flamboyantly expensive, but, in fact, it's surprisingly easy, and for the price of one portion at a restaurant you can feed yourself and five friends at home—since you're mixing it with salad and crepes, the meat goes a long way. I really wouldn't bother making the crepes yourself (none of my Chinese friends would consider doing anything so time-consuming); instead, buy them frozen and keep them on hand for whenever you choose to cook a duck. It's a good idea to keep a jar of plum sauce in the pantry, too.

I've eaten this at the legendary Quanjude restaurant in Beijing, which is world-famous for its crispy duck. There, they bring the duck to your table on its own gurney, and a silent chef in a ridiculously tall hat cuts it into 50 separate slices. If I were you, I'd forget the hat and the 50 slices; opt for the classic local Chinese restaurant approach and shred the duck using a pair of forks.

SERVES 6

1 duck, weighing 5 ½– 6 ½lb
¼ cup honey
1 tablespoon white wine
1 tablespoon dark soy sauce (or 2 tablespoons regular soy sauce)
⅔ cup hoisin or plum sauce

TO SERVE

40–50 frozen Peking duck crepes (sometimes sold as Mandarin crepes), defrosted
1 cucumber, cored and cut into very thin strips, about 4in long
8 scallions, cut lengthwise into long thin strips
plum sauce

Remove any excess fat that can be pulled from the cavity of the duck and place it in a roasting pan that will fit in your fridge. Mix the honey, wine, soy sauce, and hoisin or plum sauce together in a bowl, then pour this sauce over the duck and rub it in. Now, store the duck breast-side down in the marinade and uncovered (it needs to dry out, for at least an hour, and overnight, if possible) somewhere cool, and secure from interested cats!

Preheat the oven to 400°F. Roast the duck, uncovered, for 30 minutes, then reduce the heat to 350°F and roast for another 1 ¼ hours. Check every now and then; the skin should be crisp and brown. Cover with foil if it looks in danger of burning.

Warm the crepes according to the instructions on the package, then place them on the table. Put the shredded cucumber and scallions onto separate plates and the plum sauce into a bowl, and place everything on the table. Bring the whole duck to the table and either shred it yourself or, better still, ask one of your friends to do it, using a couple of forks. (Don't worry—you don't have to be elegant about this!) The legs are a little tricky, but persevere, since you'll need all the meat and skin to feed six people.

To make each crepe, spread a little plum sauce on it first, then add cucumber, scallions, duck meat, and skin, then roll it up and eat it.

SHABU-SHABU

Shabu-shabu is one of those meals that always seems to shine a light into my life, turning dinner into a party and making my friends lose their inhibitions. It's basically a healthy Japanese version of fondue, where you lay thin slices of fish, meat, and vegetables around the table and put a large pot of boiling stock in the middle for everyone to poach their food in. The Japanese name "shabu-shabu" refers to the sound of the food being waved from side-to-side through the water (it should be so thin that it cooks in seconds), and it's very similar to Chinese and Singaporean dishes known as steamboats. At the end of the meal, you give everyone a bowl of noodles and then pour the remaining stock over for a palate-cleansing noodle soup.

I've created this slightly untraditional version using ingredients more commonly available in Western supermarkets, although if you can lay your hands on a bottle of sesame dipping sauce and ponzu (a lemony soy sauce) that would be great (see Suppliers, page 218).

You could make elaborate dashi stock or homemade fish stock (the best I ever made was from old shrimp shells) but there's so much fun and flavor in the cooking process that all you really need is a gentle, fragrant stock (a really good bouillon cube will do), and some food to dip into it (a vegetarian version is fine, too).

ESSENTIAL GEAR

In practical terms, you do need some sort of heating device in the middle of the table for this, but it doesn't need to be a fondue set—a camp stove will happily do the trick, so long as it's stable. I use a very cheap tabletop portable gas burner, and these are widely available, as are the replacement gas canisters. Actually, I have three burners for big feasts; unless you have a circular table, one pot and burner usually only work for up to six people. If you have a larger group, your friends will be sitting too far away from the pot to be able to cook comfortably.

Chopsticks are really useful for this dish, and if you really get into Shabu-shabu, you can buy little basket/spoon utensils (they look a little like tea strainers) from Chinese supermarkets that are handy, although not really essential, since tea strainers do just as well.

SERVES 6

2 skinless chicken breasts, very thinly sliced (see method)
10oz pork fillet, very thinly sliced (see method)
14oz beef fillet, very thinly sliced (see method)
2 quarts good chicken stock, warmed to a simmer
1 large piece of kombu seaweed (optional)
8 Chinese cabbage leaves, washed and thickly sliced
1 head of broccoli, cut into small florets
3 carrots, cut into long, thin slices
6oz fresh spinach, washed
9oz mushrooms (Enoki, if available), sliced, if large
12.3oz package firm tofu, diced
10oz rice noodles, cooked according to package instructions, refreshed in cold water, and tossed in oil to keep them from clumping

FOR THE DIPPING SAUCE
½ cup soy sauce
⅓ cup superfine sugar
⅓ cup rice vinegar
4 scallions, finely chopped
4 egg yolks
½ medium-hot red chile, thinly sliced
store-bought ponzu sauce and sesame dipping sauce (optional)

Unless you're a whizz with a knife, put your meat into the freezer for 45 minutes before slicing it to help you cut it as thinly as possible. Don't worry too much about this, though—the Japanese usually buy meat precut to the thickness of bacon, but even chunks will be fine—really. This dish isn't about authenticity—it's about fun.

To make the dipping sauce, put all the sauce ingredients into a jam jar or bowl and stir thoroughly to combine. Divide it between small bowls or teacups so that everyone has dipping sauce of their own. Give everyone a plate, a set of chopsticks, a spoon, and a bowl of dipping sauce (and another of ponzu sauce or sesame dipping sauce, if using).

Place your tabletop burner or camp stove in the middle of the table; put a wide, flat pan on it (a frying pan would do in a pinch); and add the stock and kombu seaweed, if using. Arrange the meat and vegetables on several plates so that everyone can reach them. Bring the stock to a gentle simmer (skimming off any scum that might rise to the surface) and invite everyone to start cooking the meat and vegetables in the hot stock.

The meat cooks very quickly (especially if you've cut it thinly), and the beef really only needs to be waved through the simmering stock from one side to the other; cooked too long and it gets tough and rubbery. Chicken takes a little longer, as do vegetables. Adjust the temperature as you see fit—the more meat and vegetables you dip in the stock, the lower the temperature gets. Once each piece of food is cooked, it should be fished out, dipped in sauce, and eaten.

When all the meat and vegetables are finished, put some cooked noodles into individual bowls, pour over the remaining flavored stock and any stray ingredients, and serve everyone a bowl of noodle soup. Each person can add any sauces they like to their bowls.

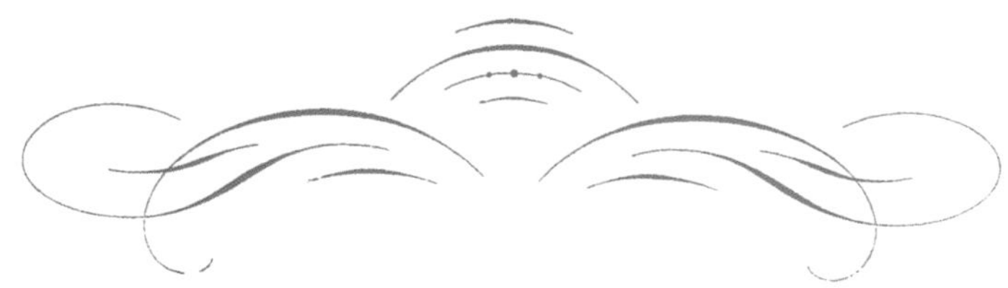

POLENTA ON THE TABLE

I do like my food to be naughty, and this is probably the naughtiest dish of all. Clear the table, wipe it down well, and then slap your polenta (or mashed potato, risotto, or a whole roast dinner, for that matter) right on top. Watch the kids' eyes light up, or your friends' mouths fall open in astonishment, then pass around the forks, and tell everyone to dig in. I guarantee that this will be another extraordinary meal that they will never forget, and with such little effort. Let's face it: You're probably going to wipe the table down after the meal anyway, and then there are all the dishes to do. Save yourself the effort and feel the exhilaration of breaking free from convention.

If you really can't bring yourself to eat straight off the table (maybe it's like our old kitchen table, with food-catching woodworm holes that hide who-knows-what), you can still enjoy a lot of the fun by using a large cutting board or two, or perhaps a tray.

SERVES 6

2¼lb Cumberland sausages (or chipolata, sweet or spicy Italian sausage, kielbasa—name your favorite)
1 red onion, finely chopped
2 tablespoons olive oil
2¾ cups polenta (instant will do, but the slow-cook version has a better texture)
2½ cups Parmesan cheese, grated
salt and freshly ground black pepper
½ tablespoon flour
½ cup red wine
⅔ cup chicken stock

Preheat the oven to 400°F. Put the sausage and chopped onion in a roasting pan that can be put on the stove later, add the oil, and stir to coat. Roast for 20 minutes (turning after 10), or until golden brown and cooked through. Don't let the onions blacken—turn the heat down, if necessary.

Meanwhile, cook the polenta according to the package instructions. When cooked through, add the Parmesan, season with salt and pepper, and stir well. Keep warm.

Remove the sausages from the roasting pan and keep warm. Pour off any excess fat from the pan, then stir the flour into the onions and put the pan on the stove over medium heat. Add the wine to the pan, stir in, and let it bubble for 4 minutes. Add the stock and simmer for about 5 minutes, until you have a nice thick gravy.

Spoon one or two big pools of polenta onto a clean table (or cutting boards if you can't bear to eat straight off the table), lay the sausages in the middle, and pour just enough gravy over the top to lubricate it, but not so much that you create a messy pool. Pass out the forks and encourage your friends to go for it!

6 SPECTACULAR MAINS

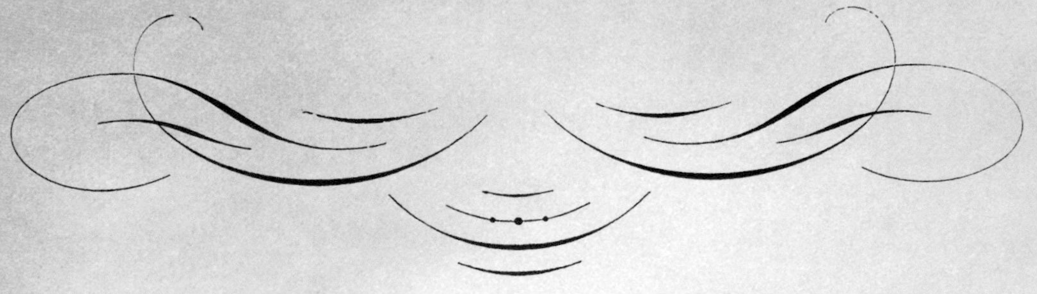

When you're ready to create a meal that your friends will never forget, you don't need lots of money, lots of skill, or even lots of food. You just need love, inspiration, and the will to do something a little different. Many of the recipes in this book are ways of reinventing the eating experience to get people playing with their food and joining in the exhilaration of communal cooking, but sometimes I just feel like cooking a meal that hits the table like a sunburst. Sometimes I want my friends to feel that dinner has turned into a feast and that this is a moment that will stay in their memories forever. So I humbly offer you these spectacular dishes, with the simple intention of taking your friends' breath away.

LEMONY CRAYFISH BARBECUED ON A FLOWERPOT

The United States is home to hundreds of varieties of crayfish (or crawfish or crawdads, depending on where you happen to be). Common varieties include the signal crayfish, found in abundance west of the Rockies, the rusty crayfish, from the Great Lakes region, and the red swamp crayfish, native to Louisiana. A few are saltwater types, but the vast majority live in freshwater.

What they all have in common is that they taste great. They're also relatively easy to catch using either a tubular, round trap or a boxy, square one. (Trapping laws vary from state to state, so check regulations in your area before you set off crayfish hunting.) Traps can be had from bait shops pretty cheaply or bought online. You just need to puncture a few holes in a can of cat food with a screwdriver, then leave it inside the trap. If you invite crayfish thus, they will come.

You don't *need* to use a flowerpot to barbecue crayfish, but it adds an extra element of fun, and flowerpots are surprisingly effective barbecues. The smoke is important for the flavor and the freezing/boiling method is a humane killing technique. If you're using a flowerpot, make sure it isn't cracked and that the hole at the bottom of the pot is clear so that air can get to your charcoal (I stand mine on three pieces of brick to make sure the air can flow into it). You can put a little grate halfway down the pot for the charcoal to rest on to make things burn better, but it's not essential.

crayfish (or shrimp)—as many as you can lay your hands on
olive oil
salt
parsley
lemon wedges

Leave freshly caught crayfish in a bucket of fresh water for 24 hours, changing the water a few times to purge them (to be honest, I don't do this, but you probably should). We should give crayfish the respect that all living creatures deserve and kill them humanely. With this in mind, place them in a secure container and put this in the freezer for 45 minutes, since this has a numbing effect on the little guys. Bring a large pan of water to a rolling boil and drop the chilled crayfish in. Put a lid on, turn the heat up as high as it will go to bring the pan back to a boil, and cook for 3 minutes, and no more.

Toss the cooked crayfish in a few splashes of olive oil just to coat them, then place them on a hot barbecue. Drop some leaves on the coals to whip up a little smoke, and let them char a little, but don't cook for more than 4–5 minutes, or they'll dry out.

Place the barbecued crayfish on a cutting board and sprinkle with salt, parsley, and a few squeezes of lemon, then dig in. Pull off the tails to find the biggest chunks of meat, but if the claws are big enough, you can crack them with the back of a knife or a hammer and find some sweet meat there, too.

BARBECUED SHRIMP

Flowerpot barbecuing is also a great way to cook shrimp. If you are using raw shrimp, simply toss them in a few splashes of olive oil, then place them on the barbecue. Make sure that they have turned from gray to pink all the way through before eating. This will take between 3–9 minutes, depending on their size.

If your shrimp are pink, they have already been cooked and just need to be warmed through on the barbecue for 2–3 minutes. Don't overcook them, or they will be rubbery.

Serve sprinkled with salt, parsley, and a few squeezes of lemon.

506 316
1932

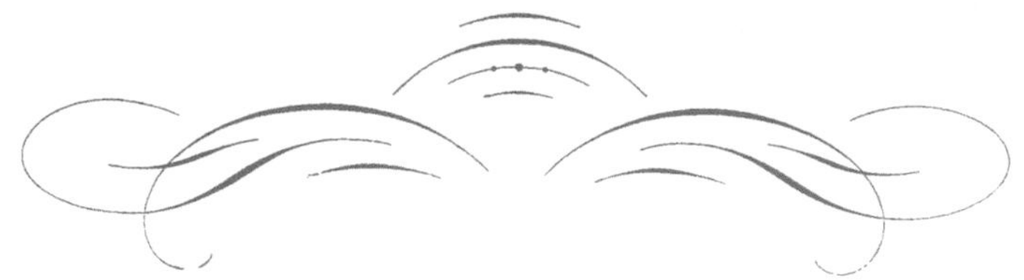

BARBECUED OYSTERS

One of the best afternoons of my life was spent trudging through the silt off Whitstable, England, gathering oysters with my friends Anneka and Angus and our assorted kids. We collected about 30 huge oysters and carried them back to their beach hut. The very largest could be opened only with a screwdriver and a hammer, but when it finally yielded, it revealed not one, but *four* pearls. Admittedly, they were little bigger than match heads, but I've eaten countless oysters in my life and not one has ever given me so much as a hint of rotund grit before. The wonderful element of hope that sprinkles a faint stardust over each and every one of these bivalves has been revived!

Oysters are magical little bivalves, but I know that some people are put off by them, either because they have a difficult time opening oysters or because they are squeamish about eating raw seafood. The great thing about barbecuing is that it solves both of those problems at once.

Just place your whole, unopened oysters on the grill rack of a good, red-hot barbecue and sit back. (Be wary of putting them directly on the coals; in my experience, oysters drip water out of their shells before they pop open, which can make the charcoal spit dangerously.)

In about 4–8 minutes (depending on the obstinacy of your bivalves), they will pop their lids open by half an inch or so, having gently poached in their own sweet, salty water. Remove from the heat as they open and allow then to cool for a minute or two, then pull the upper shell off completely and eat the delicious nugget that lies within.

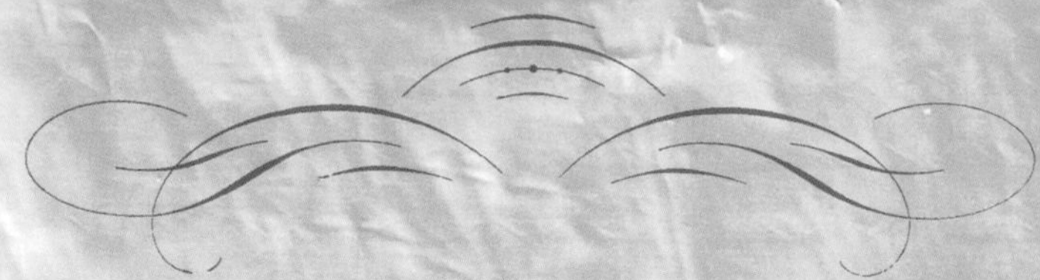

HERB FISH PARCELS

This is a fantastic way to cook fish, and it works with all kinds of flavor combinations. It's easy and quick to make, but it's also a lovely dish to receive because you feel as though you've been given a present to unwrap. I like adding an element of surprise by using different flavorings in each parcel so that no one knows what they're getting until they tuck in. Take your pick from the basic flavorings and other favorites of mine listed below, or invent your own.

The basic method is the same for all: oil and season some foil, add the fish and some herbs or other flavorings, splash on some liquid, and wrap up. After the parcels have been baked, your friends open them up on their plates, the flavors rise up in a cloud of steam, and the amalgamated liquids in the parcels make a great sauce.

This way of cooking works well with lots of different fish, too. My favorites are whole gilt-head bream, small bass, trout, mackerel, and sole. I prefer to serve them with their heads on, but it's up to you. If you're using fillets, pretty much any fish will do, but flat fish or salmon fillets are particularly good.

SERVES 6

olive oil
salt and freshly ground black pepper
6 small, whole mackerel, trout, bass, or bream; descaled and gutted

BASIC FLAVORINGS (AMOUNTS FOR 6 SERVINGS)
a large handful of fresh thyme
6 rosemary sprigs
1 lemon, cut into slices
1 large garlic clove, crushed
1 ¼ cups white wine

Preheat the oven to 375°F. Lay down a piece of foil for each fish (it should be about twice the length of the fish and four times as wide). In the middle of each piece of foil, coat an area twice the size of the fish with olive oil, then sprinkle with plenty of salt and pepper. Lay the cleaned fish in the middle of the foil and add your chosen herbs and flavorings, putting about half inside the cavity and laying the other half on top and around the fish. Bring up the sides of the foil a bit, add a splash of wine (or other liquid), and then close the parcel, folding the ends over to seal it loosely. There's no great art to the wrapping, but try to make sure that the foil is not all bunched up on top, or the fish won't heat through evenly.

Lay the parcels on a baking sheet and bake in the oven for about 15–20 minutes (small, whole fish) or 25 minutes (larger, whole-fish parcels to serve 2 people). Check that they are cooked through, then place the parcels on individual plates, and let your friends unwrap them themselves. Serve with lemon couscous or herb rice.

OTHER FLAVORING OPTIONS

1 cup coconut milk
large handful of chopped cilantro leaves and stems
splash of fish sauce
splash of soy sauce

1 large thumb of ginger, thinly sliced
large handful of chopped cilantro
1 ¼ cups white wine

1 fennel bulb with fronds, thinly sliced
½–¾ cups vermouth (don't use too much, or it will overpower the fish)

12 bay leaves
3 large garlic cloves, thinly sliced
1 ¼ cups white wine

large handful of chopped parsley leaves
3 large garlic cloves, thinly sliced
1 lemon, cut into slices
1 ¼ cups white wine

WHOLE BAKED FISH

I know I keep saying this, but spectacular food doesn't need to be complicated, and baking a whole large fish is a perfect illustration of this. When you place a huge, whole fish on the table, simply cooked, its skin crisp and its flesh moist and fragrant, you're likely to earn a round of applause despite a shocking lack of effort on your part. It's all in the vision rather than the work, so be bold, and you'll lay on a spread fit for a king within an hour of getting home from work.

Now, you could cook a six-person John Dory—if you're lucky enough to find one and your wallet can stretch to it—although wild striped bass, Arctic char, and red snapper are equally delicious. If you've managed to plan ahead (in which case you're infinitely more organized than I am), you could order the fish to ensure that you have a whole fish of your choice that's large enough to feed your friends. Otherwise, ask for advice at the fish counter as to how large a fish you'll need and what's the freshest and best that day.

The technique is essentially the same for all these fish, although they do take to different herbs, if you like experimenting. The yield of John Dory is less than many others, but the intensity of its flavor seems to make up for this. I recently tried this recipe with Dover sole, and it was outrageously good.

SERVES 6

olive oil
8 fresh thyme sprigs
1 tablespoon fresh rosemary leaves
3½lb whole fish (e.g., John Dory, wild striped bass, Arctic char, red snapper, sole—1 large fish, if possible), gutted and descaled, head on
½ cup butter, cut into small chunks
salt and freshly ground black pepper
a small handful of parsley
1 lemon, cut into segments

Preheat the oven to 425°F. Spread a pool of olive oil on a large, low-sided baking sheet, then scatter half the herbs on it, and lay the whole fish on top, its eyes facing upward if you're cooking a flat fish. Scatter the rest of the thyme and rosemary over the fish and dot all over with small chunks of butter. Season liberally with salt and pepper.

Bake uncovered in the oven for 20–35 minutes (this depends on the thickness of your fish), until the skin is crispy and the flesh is opaque but still moist. Remove from the oven, scatter the parsley on top, and place the whole baking sheet in the middle of the table (put it on a large cutting board, if that's easier), along with the lemon. Let your friends dig into the fish themselves, separating the fillets from the bones, and, if necessary, spooning out the juices to use as a sauce.

Serve with crusty bread, creamy mashed potatoes or sautéed potatoes, and some crunchy green beans.

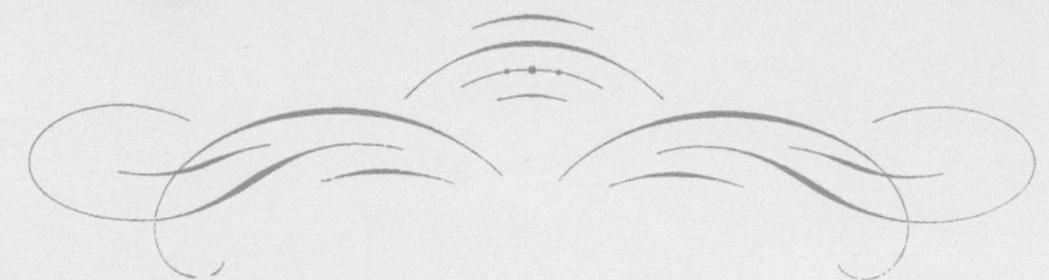

ROASTED FISH HEADS

It's well-known that fish and meat stay moist and tender when cooked on the bone, and this principle is taken to its ultimate manifestation when you cook large fish heads. While the prized part of a chicken is the little "oyster" tucked underneath the base (which I always steal when carving), the best morsel from a fish is the cheek, situated just under the skin between the eyes and gills. But all the other meat that rests against and around the head is delicious, too.

This dish is very handy if you're feeling the financial pinch but want to lay on a spectacular spread for your friends. You can use any large fish head—I've used conger eel heads in the past, which were sublime—and the fishmonger may even give them to you for free if you're buying other fish at the same time. I often pick up a few particularly meaty heads when I spot them at the fish market, then pop them in the freezer for a rainy day. If you're paying for the heads, ask that a little extra meat be left on the shoulders. Salmon, cod, and large pollack are good for this dish, and I once managed to salvage a very large John Dory head, which was excellent. The Spanish make this with hake heads, and the tongues are a great delicacy.

You'll need to use your (or your fishmonger's) best judgment as to how many heads you'll need, but as a rough guide, a small head from a fish weighing up to 4½lb will serve one, a larger head from a fish weighing 4½–9lb will serve two people, and a whopper may be enough for four.

SERVES 6

6 medium fish heads
2 lemons, sliced
olive oil
salt and freshly ground black pepper
6 large garlic cloves, roughly chopped
6 thyme sprigs
a handful of fresh rosemary leaves

Preheat the oven to 425°F. Rinse the heads, pat them dry with paper towels, then, using a sharp knife, make a few slashes in the skin of each one. Lay half the lemon slices on a baking sheet, then lay the fish heads on top. Pour a generous amount of olive oil over each head, then season with plenty of salt and pepper and half of the garlic, and rub into the skin. Push a few leaves of thyme and rosemary into each slash of the skin, put a few in the mouth and gill-vents, and tuck any remaining ones under the fish. Scatter the remaining herbs and garlic over the top and pour some more oil over to make sure the fish heads are well lubricated.

Bake, uncovered, in the oven for 20–45 minutes, depending on the size of the heads.

Serve, garnished with the remaining lemon slices, with rice or couscous and a salad.

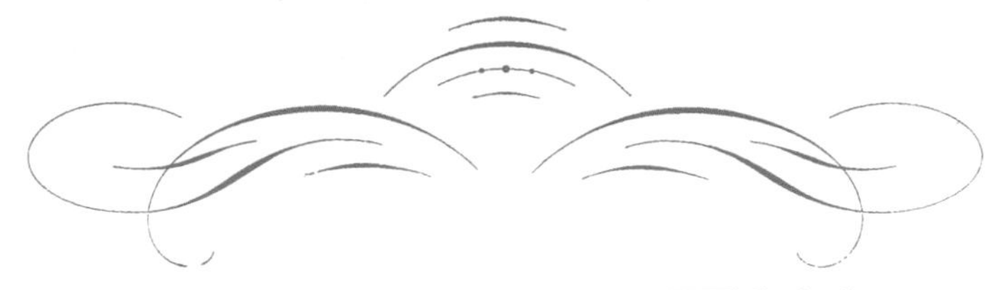

COOKIE-TIN SMOKED SALMON

Hot-smoking is a rudimentary and slightly magical way to cook that's so simple you won't quite believe it works until you try it. Just a handful of hardwood shavings and a handful of herbs are enough both to cook and smoke the fish, giving it a very different, more noticeably smoky taste than the cold-smoked salmon you're familiar with, and a surprisingly delicate texture. Kids especially love the theater of hot-smoking, and if you want to make them "ooh" and "aah," you can create plumes of smoke by pulling the lid off the tin while it's still on the heat. If you're being much more grown-up about the whole affair, or are in danger of setting off the smoke alarm, just let the tin cool after cooking. Despite the photo here (I got a bit carried away), you can do this in your kitchen without smoking the place out, providing you switch on the stove's extractor fan.

The wood chips and herbs inside the tin start to smolder within seconds of putting the tin over a flame and the heat cooks the fish in just 3–8 minutes (depending on the thickness of the fillet and the heat source), while the smoke swirls around in convection currents, giving it a deep, smokehouse flavor. The first time you try this you'll probably be tempted to cook the salmon for longer, but trust me—test after 3 minutes and try to retain a little pinkness in the middle. If you smoke it for too long, the flavor will be overpowering.

I've used the tin in the photo for seven years now, and it's survived everything from camp fires to gas burners—it's light, handy to carry, and it never needs more than a quick scrubbing. I've added bolts as handles for the lid and base to make things easier, but you don't really need them. You can happily substitute mackerel fillets for this recipe—but bear in mind that they take even less time to cook.

GEAR

- a length of unpainted chicken wire, an old grill rack, or a piece of metal mesh (mine is cut from an old disposable barbecue)
- 1 large cookie tin
- a few large handfuls of hardwood or fruitwood chips (not pine or coated wood, since this leaves a resinous taste). If in doubt, buy some from a garden center, or see Suppliers, page 218.

SERVES 4

- 2 handfuls of rosemary, thyme, and/or bay leaves, preferably on the branch
- vegetable oil for brushing
- 1 ¾lb salmon fillet (removed from the fridge 15 minutes before use)
- salt and freshly ground black pepper

Using chicken wire or metal mesh, make a little grill rack to fit inside the tin, curled around so it will support a hunk of fish an inch or two above the base. (You can use a bundle of chicken wire, basically, as long as the top is relatively flat.) If you want to, add crude handles to the tin using one bolt jammed into the lid and another on the side of the base (you don't *need* these, but they do make life a little easier).

Scatter a handful of wood chips and herbs in the bottom of the tin, then brush the grill rack with oil to stop the fish from sticking. Season the fish, then place it on the rack. Put the lid firmly on the tin, then place it over high heat. (A little smoke may escape, but don't worry.) Cook for 3 minutes (small fillets), then remove the tin from the heat (watch out—it will be very hot), and check that it's cooked. Cook for a few minutes more, if necessary, adding more wood chips as needed; don't overcook, however, since the whole beauty of the dish is its moist delicacy contrasted with its strong flavor.

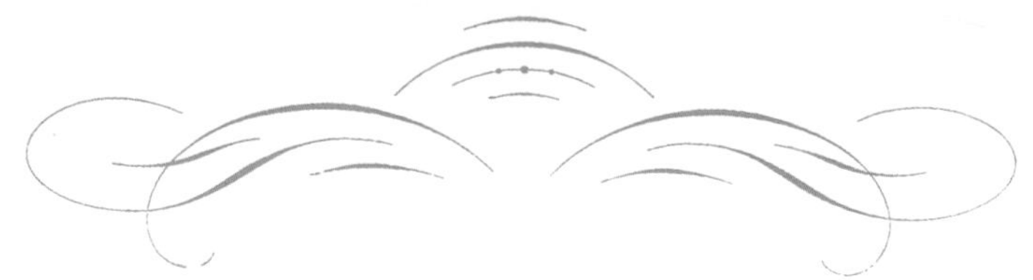

LUNCH COOKED IN THE DISHWASHER

Yes, you really can poach salmon—and the rest of your lunch—in a dishwasher and, no, it doesn't end up tasting like soap! Dishwashers heat their water during the cycle and that heat is enough to poach salmon and gently infuse it with the flavors of aromatic herbs. My dishwasher runs a 130–150°F cycle, which makes the most meltingly delicious poached salmon, and also makes extraordinary asparagus that's very crunchy, yet oddly tender, too. The trick is to keep your fish wrapped tightly in foil, skip the detergent, and run the dishwasher on the highest and hottest cycle.

You don't have to use an empty dishwasher, but neither would I put anything particularly dirty in it, in case of contamination. By the way, other household appliances that can be employed to cook food—provided you use them with caution—are hairdryers (good for cooking pizza, although it takes a long time), steel log-burners (make fantastic pizza ovens), security lights (you can just about cook crepes on them), and irons (great for cooking bacon).

SERVES 6

FOR THE SALMON PARCEL
olive oil
2¼lb salmon fillet, skinned and pin-boned
zest and juice of 2 fresh limes
a large thumb of ginger, peeled and thinly sliced into rounds
a large handful of cilantro, finely chopped
salt and freshly ground black pepper

FOR THE ASPARAGUS PARCEL
1 bunch of asparagus
a pat of butter
salt and freshly ground black pepper

FOR THE NOODLE PARCEL
1 14oz package of fresh noodles
2 scallions, finely sliced
1 teaspoon toasted sesame oil
1 teaspoon Thai fish sauce (nam pla)

FOR THE TWO MIXED VEGETABLE PARCELS
1 red pepper, cored, deseeded, and finely sliced
1lb bean sprouts
1 teaspoon toasted sesame oil
10oz bok choy (Chinese cabbage), chopped into thick slices
a few thin slices of mild red chile
1 tablespoon soy sauce

Place five double layers of foil, each 12in square, on the work surface. Drizzle some oil onto each square of foil and spread it over the surface using a pastry brush.

Put the salmon fillet in the middle of one square and fold up the edges of the foil a little to make a bowl. Sprinkle with the lime zest and juice, place the ginger slices on top, then scatter the cilantro over everything, and season. Bring the sides of the foil together, pinching to make a watertight package.

Follow the same method for the asparagus and noodle parcels, and divide the vegetables between two more parcels, ensuring that the parcels are flat rather than round, or the heat won't get to the food long enough for it to cook. Place your packages on the top rack of the dishwasher, choose the hottest and longest cycle (the parcels should cook for about 1 hour), and don't add any detergent!

At the end of the cycle, remove the parcels. Unwrap the parcels at the table and let everyone dig in.

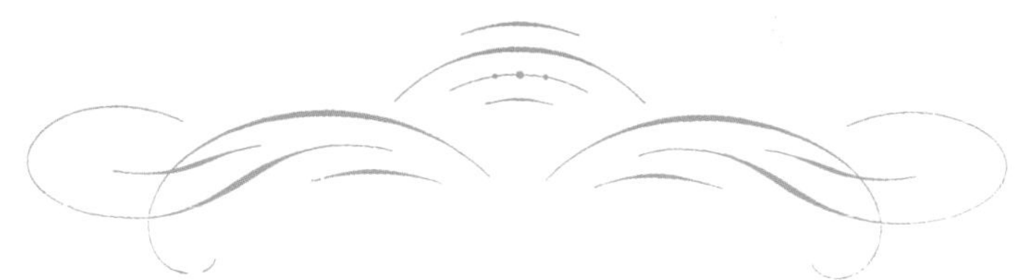

TEN-MINUTE SASHIMI COURSE

Yes, I really am going to cherry-pick from the Japanese chef's seven hard years of training to teach you how to make the finest sashimi in a mere 10 minutes. Just to be clear, it'll take you a little longer actually to make it (the rice takes an hour), but I think you'll be surprised at how easy it is when you strip sashimi back to the core elements. Ten minutes of reading this should provide you with the basics, and I'd urge you to read all the way through before you begin, so that you know what's involved. I make sashimi at least once a week, usually when I'm feeling lazy yet gastronautically inclined, and my family and friends always love it.

Sashimi is raw fish, sliced and served alongside sushi rice. The key thing is to buy sparklingly fresh fish that smells of the sea and nothing else—remember to tell the fishmonger that you'll be using it for sashimi, so that you get the very best. To keep things simple, we're going to make salmon, mackerel, squid, and scallop sashimi, which are easy to prepare and cheap (as long as you don't buy too many scallops), but still among the finest food on the planet. Once you've got the hang of it, you could try sea bass, red snapper, and more. (However, I really think it's time we gave tuna a rest, before there's none left.) Oh, and don't buy fish on a Monday—fishermen don't usually work on Sundays, so freshness will be compromised.

So, this is what's going to happen: You marinate the mackerel in a vinegar mixture while you cut the salmon, squid, and scallops and arrange them on a plate; then serve everything with wasabi and side bowls of sushi rice. The squid is a little chewy, so you might want to cut it into wafer-thin slices.

Tip: For beautiful fish-cutting, use a long, sharp knife, freshly sharpened.

SERVES 6

18oz best salmon fillet (buy loin, if it's available), skinned and pin-boned
2 medium mackerel, each filleted into 2 pieces
6 fat scallops
1 medium-sized squid, cleaned and prepared at the fish counter, if possible, with the tentacles reserved
1 tablespoon wasabi powder

TO SERVE

soy or shoyu sauce (see note on page 124)
Wasabi powder (or English mustard or freshly grated horseradish)
Sake, pickled ginger, and a selection of Japanese or Chinese pickled vegetables (optional)

FOR THE RICE

3 cups sushi rice
½ cup rice vinegar
5 tablespoons superfine sugar (or mirin)
3 teaspoons salt
(the above 3 ingredients can be replaced by ¾ cup preseasoned sushi rice vinegar, if you've bought it)

FOR MARINATING THE MACKEREL

¼ cup salt
¼ cup superfine sugar
1 cup rice vinegar

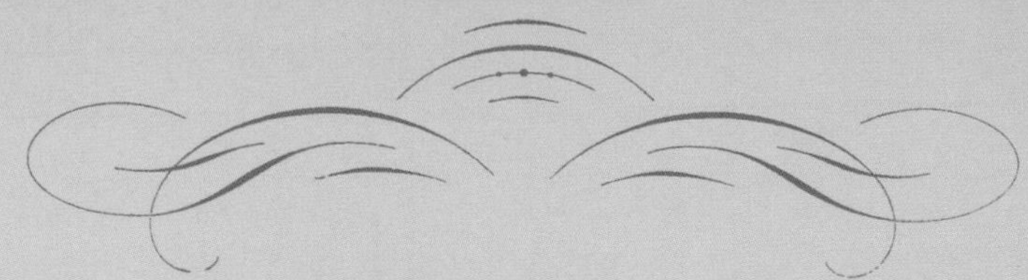

HERB-AND-SALT-CRUST BAKED CHICKEN

This recipe has magic and drama in spades. It's amazing to see a whole chicken arrive at the table encased in an armor of herbs and salt and to smell the intensity of the flavors as they burst forth when you crack it open. The salt crust acts as a seal, keeping the flavorings close to the skin as the chicken steams within. You'll need to throw all the salt away once the bird is cooked—and do be careful as you crack the crust open so the salt doesn't mix too much with the meat. Bear in mind that you won't get any useable juices from the chicken when it's cooked in this way.

SERVES 4

3½lb free-range chicken
2¼lb coarse salt or rock salt
1 lemon, zested, juiced, and rinds reserved
a large handful of rosemary leaves, chopped
1 tablespoon thyme leaves
4 garlic cloves, thinly sliced
4 bay leaves

Preheat the oven to 400°F. Rinse the chicken, but leave it trussed, and pat dry. In a large bowl, mix the salt together with the lemon zest and juice and half the rosemary, thyme, and garlic. Add just enough water to make it damp—it should have the consistency of seaside-castle-building sand.

Push the lemon rinds into the chicken cavity, ensuring that you close it up afterward. Line a roasting pan with foil, then lay a bed of salt, using about a quarter of what's in your bowl, over its base. Place the bay leaves on the salt, then put the chicken on top. Scatter the remaining herbs and garlic on top of the chicken, and then pack the rest of the salt around it until it's well covered. Cover everything with another layer of foil.

Bake for 1½ hours, then remove the pan from the oven and carefully peel back the foil. Bring the pan to the table and break open the salt crust to reveal the chicken inside. Break off and discard all the salt, then carve the chicken and serve with potatoes and vegetables and perhaps a lemony/garlicky gravy.

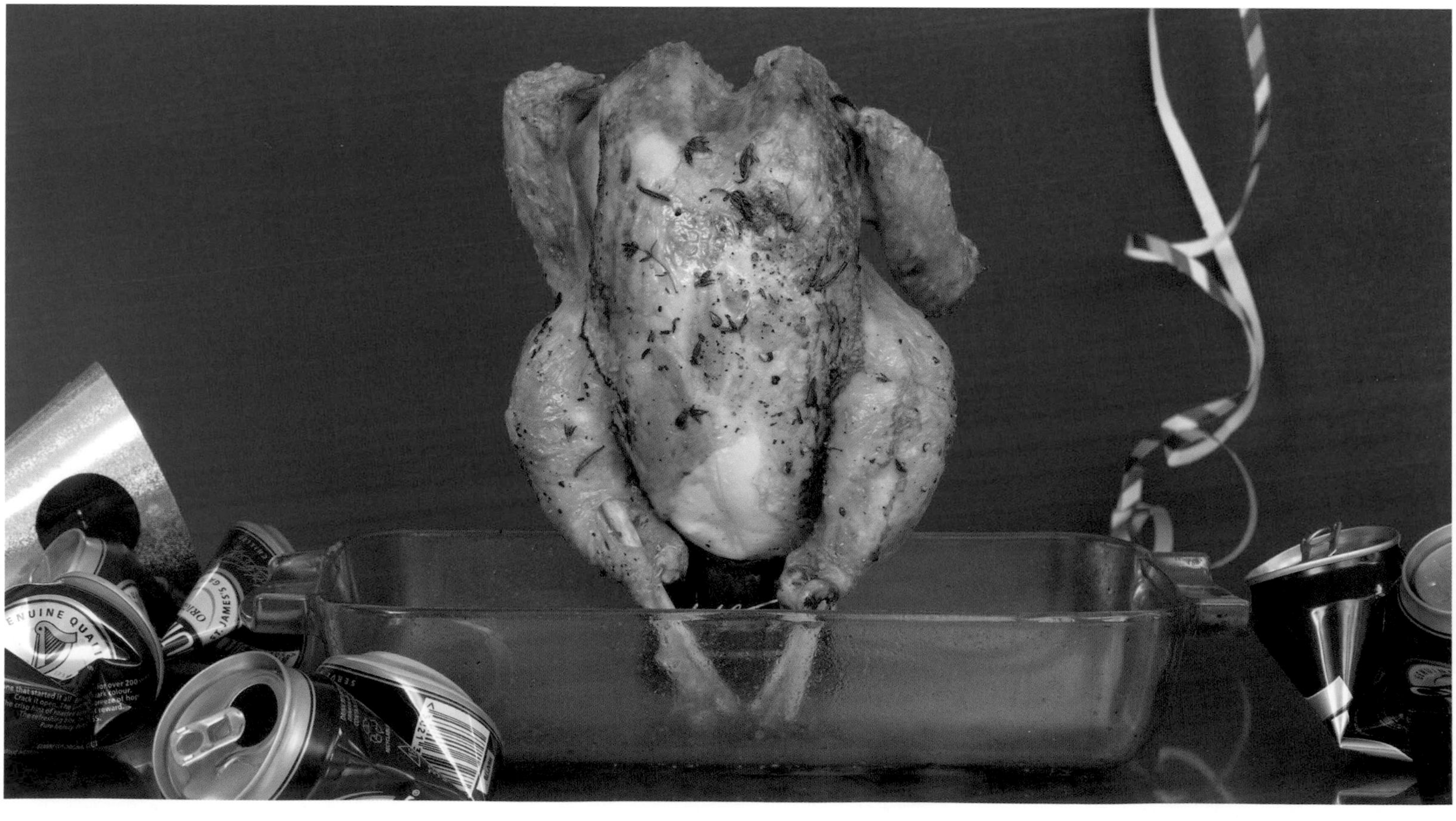

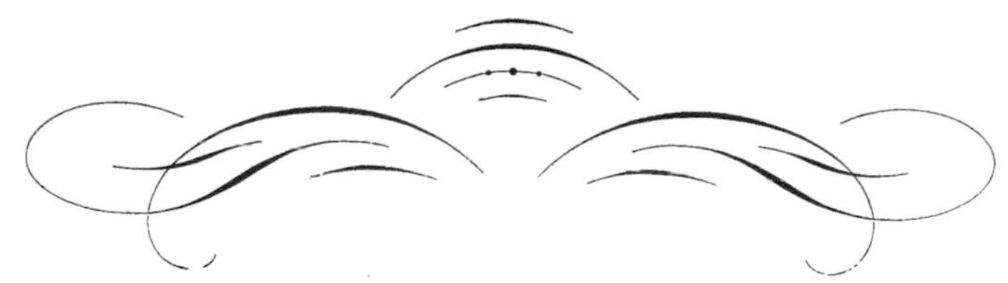

BEER-CAN CHICKEN

It looks a little startling, but there is a good culinary reason for sticking a can of beer up a chicken's rear end—the beer steams the chicken inside, while the heat from the oven cooks and crisps up the outside. This dual approach stops the bird from drying out and leaves you with a moist and tasty baked chicken. This way of cooking a chicken works well in the oven, but not so well on the barbecue, unless you start off by cooking the top of the chicken, then turn it over, and arrange the bird on the can.

You can experiment with your favorite flavors—I like using a can of hard cider because the sweetness and apple flavoring are delicious, and cider makes a lovely gravy. The one in the picture uses Guinness, because my wife, Georgia, loves the stuff, but it's no good for gravy, since it tastes too bitter. Pilsner beers and ales are pretty good, too. If you want something nonalcoholic, a can of ginger ale or lemonade works just as well.

3 ½lb free-range chicken
1 tablespoon olive oil
salt and freshly ground black pepper
1 tablespoon chopped rosemary
1 tablespoon chopped thyme
12oz can of your favorite beer, hard cider, or soft drink; room temperature

Preheat the oven to 400°F. Wipe the chicken inside and out, then trickle the oil all over it, season with plenty of salt and pepper, and scatter the herbs on top. Using your hands, rub the oily herb mixture all over the chicken. Tuck the wings behind the chicken to keep them from burning.

Drink or pour out half the can of beer, then place it on a roasting pan. Push the chicken onto the open can and make sure it's firmly balanced and won't fall over (if it's unstable, place the whole thing on an ovenproof bowl for balance). Cover the top of the chicken with a piece of foil to keep it from drying out, then roast in the oven for about 1 ¼ hours, turning the heat down to 350°F after the first 45 minutes.

Remove the chicken from the oven and check that it's cooked through, then cover with foil and leave to rest for 15 minutes. Remove the can (be careful, since it may still be very hot) and carve.

Serve with gravy, roasted potatoes, and vegetables.

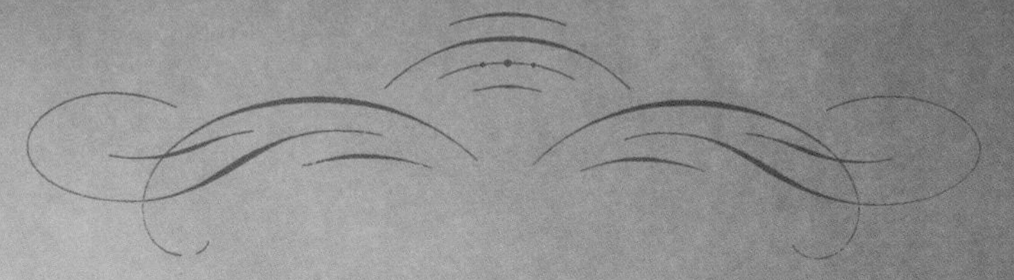

GOLDEN CHICKEN

One thing is certain: If you cook golden chicken for your friends, they will never, ever forget it. You'll also be pleasantly surprised to find that it's easy to make and not as expensive as you might think. I've been gilding food for years—mostly sausages and chocolates for the sheer excitement they cause, especially for kids. The difference with this gilded chicken is not just the extraordinary spectacle, but also its taste, because it just so happens that the best cooking method for chicken-gilding is also an absurdly easy way to make the moistest, most tender chicken imaginable, using the simple *poule au pot* method of gently poaching the chicken together with some vegetables. You can make this in advance and keep (or reheat) it in the oven to retain the element of surprise.

I'd be crazy to ignore the glaringly profligate, materialistic symbolism of eating gold, so it's only right that I offer you some ideas for justifying your extravagance to your guests, should you feel the need to do so. The first justification is that gold leaf is so thin that only a microscopic amount is needed to gild a whole chicken, costing perhaps half the price of a bottle of Champagne. And hey, you're not going to eat gold every day—that would be tacky. Second, this is celebration food with an ancient pedigree that often features at Indian weddings and on candies and chocolates. Your third justification is simply this: "Oh my God, look! It's a golden chicken! Oh my God!"

GOLD LEAF

Gold is odorless and tasteless, and gold leaf has been beaten to the thickness of a few atoms, which means that it doesn't react on metal fillings like aluminum foil does. It's safe to eat—it's a permitted food additive with its own E number (E175—silver is E174).

You can buy gold leaf in booklets from either art supplier stores, edible decoration suppliers, or online, but I'd shop around, since the prices vary wildly. Check how many leaves are in the book and what size they are. You're looking for transfer leaf of at least 23 carat purity, which comes in books of 12 or 25 leaves, each pressed against a leaf of tissue paper. Loose leaf is a little trickier to handle, and gold powder is extremely expensive.

3 ½lb free-range chicken
1 medium onion, peeled and halved
bouquet garni made from 5 flat-leaf parsley stems, 3 thyme sprigs, and 3 bay leaves, tied together with string
2 cups chicken stock (fresh or made with a chicken bouillion cube)
salt and freshly ground black pepper
1 ¼lb baby new potatoes, scrubbed
1 ¼lb carrots, scrubbed but whole
a handful of baby onions, peeled
small turnips or chopped parsnips (optional)
a pat of butter
about 12 leaves of edible parchment gold

If your chicken is trussed, keep it like that to retain its shape. Stuff the halved onion into the breast cavity, and put the chicken in a saucepan or casserole dish large enough to fit the vegetables, too. Add cold water until the chicken is completely submerged, then add the bouquet garni and chicken stock and season with salt and pepper. Place the pan over medium heat and slowly bring to a simmer.

Skim and dispose of any scum that rises to the surface, then put the lid on the pan and lower the heat. Simmer gently for 35 minutes, then add the potatoes and carrots—plus the baby onions, turnips, and parsnips, if using—and simmer for another 15 minutes.

Place the chicken on a carving platter and test that it's cooked (the juices in the thigh should run clear when pricked with a skewer). Cover, and leave to rest for 10 minutes.

Check the vegetables for tenderness and cook for a few more minutes, if necessary; otherwise, remove them from the stock to serving dishes, toss them in butter, season to taste, and keep warm. Pour away all but 2 cups of the liquid from the pan, then return the pan to the heat and reduce by about half to use as gravy.

Now, for the gilding. Wipe excess moisture from the chicken with paper towels (although the skin will need to remain a little damp and sticky for the gold to stick), then simply press the gold transfer leaf against the chicken. The gold should come off and stick to the skin. If you need to remoisten the skin, dab it with a little of the cooking liquid, using paper towels or a pastry brush. You can use a small paintbrush to help fix the gold leaf in place, but don't handle it or it will come off on your fingers. It's tricky, but fun! When you've finished, you can keep the chicken warm in the oven, covered with a dome of foil or another roasting pan sat upside-down, but try not to let anything touch the gold.

Cook some broccoli or peas to accompany the chicken. When you are ready to serve, put the gravy into a gravy boat, arrange the gilded bird on the middle of a platter, and surround it with the vegetables. Then, bring it to the table with a confused look on your face.

VARIATIONS

This is an excellent way to cook chicken, whether you gild it or not. You could also try using pure silver leaf, too, which is a quarter of the price of gold… although this might be missing a trick.

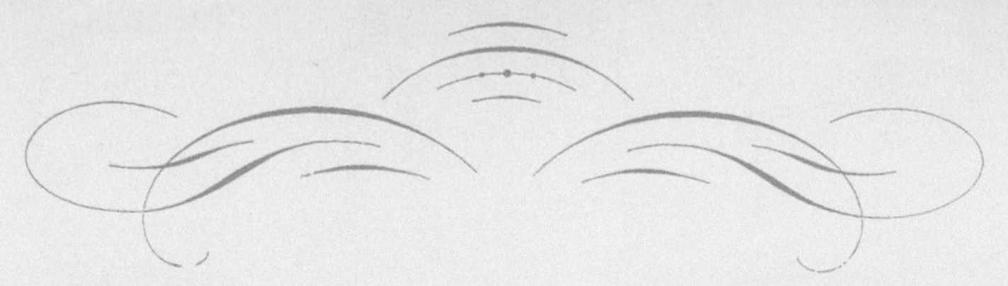

RABBIT IN CREAMY MUSTARD SAUCE

The British are extremely sentimental about rabbits, so there's always an element of spectacle when they arrive at a table in the form of lunch, but across most of Continental Europe, rabbit is a highly prized dish and fetches a good price at the butcher shop. The reason for this contrast in attitudes is unclear—French kids love a cuddly *lapin* as much as English tykes. I think it's all down to Beatrix Potter, who so thoroughly anthropomorphized the rabbit that eating one is a bit like eating your childhood sweetheart. But, whatever the reason, the result is that Brits eat few rabbits now, so fewer are hunted and they are left to party on the juicy crops of this pleasant land.

Rabbits have little fat on them, so they are a healthy meat if you're feeling fulsome, (although this also means they can dry out if overcooked); they taste like slightly gamey chicken; they are cheap; and they have an unfamiliar bone structure if you're used to carving chicken, with quite a few little bones. If you can get your hands on enough rabbit livers, they also make an excellent variation on the chicken liver parfait on page 54. Oh, and this recipe is also fantastic with chicken.

SERVES 6

10 garlic cloves, roughly chopped
4 tablespoons Dijon mustard
2 tablespoons fresh thyme leaves
8 bay leaves
salt and freshly ground black pepper
5 tablespoons olive oil
2 medium-size rabbits, each jointed into 4 legs and 3 or 4 sections of saddle (see picture, left)
2 onions, finely sliced
1 cup heavy cream
⅓ cup white wine or chicken stock
1 teaspoon sugar

Preheat the oven to 375°F. In a small bowl, mix together the garlic, mustard, thyme, bay leaves, salt and pepper, and 3 tablespoons of the olive oil. Rub this pungent mixture all over your rabbit pieces and lay them in a roasting pan. Bake uncovered for 25 minutes.

Meanwhile, put a frying pan over low to medium heat and add 2 tablespoons of olive oil and the onion. Fry gently until softened and translucent, then add the cream, wine or stock, and sugar to the pan and warm gently over low heat. Remove the rabbit from the oven, stir the sauce and pour over the rabbit, making sure it's thoroughly coated, then return the pan to the oven for another 20 minutes.

Serve the rabbit with the sauce and some boiled potatoes, or if you're feeling fancy, a parsnip or celery root gratin.

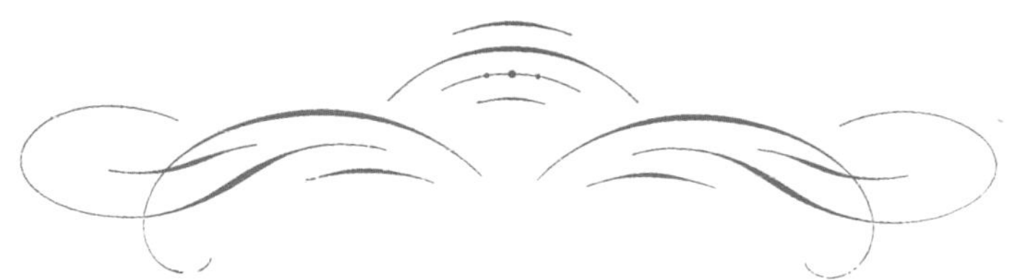

SAUTÉED SWEETBREADS ON BRIOCHE

The name "sweetbread" is often thought—incorrectly—to be a euphemism for "testicle." In fact, sweetbreads can come from one of two different glands: the thymus glands (near the throat) and the pancreatic glands (near the stomach). The most prized are from calves, but lambs' sweetbreads are also delicious. Creamy and delicate, I think they would be much more commonly eaten at home were it not for the fact that many recipes tell you to soak them for ages before you cook them, although in reality, soaking for a brief period seems to make no perceptible difference. Although this recipe takes a little time, the process is very simple. Just bear in mind that you may need to order your sweetbreads in advance, unless your butcher is pretty upmarket or serves a lamb-loving ethnic group.

SERVES 6

2¾lb sweetbreads
all-purpose flour, for dusting
salt and freshly ground black pepper
2 tablespoons olive oil
9oz smoked bacon, chopped into chunks
3 large garlic cloves, finely chopped
1 tablespoon fresh thyme leaves
2 tablespoons red currant jelly (or other good fruit jelly)
1 tablespoon white wine vinegar
1½ cups beef stock (kept warm in a pan)
small handful of chopped parsley
a large pat of butter
6 fat slices of brioche (one large loaf)

Soak the sweetbreads in a large pan of cold water while you prepare your other ingredients.

Bring a large pan of water to a simmer, then add the sweetbreads and simmer very gently for 3–4 minutes. Remove with a slotted spoon, place on some paper towels, and leave to cool.

Pick the sweetbreads over, removing any gristle and peeling away any thicker exterior membrane using a sharp knife. (Don't worry about the thinner membranes; they help hold the sweetbread together.)

Spread out a couple of handfuls of flour on a plate and season it with plenty of salt and pepper, then gently toss the sweetbreads in it. Heat the oil in a large frying pan over medium heat, then add the bacon and fry for 5 minutes, stirring occasionally. Add the sweetbreads, sprinkle the garlic and thyme over the top, and fry for 2 minutes on one side. Turn the sweetbreads over and continue frying, stirring to make sure nothing sticks or burns, until they are golden and crisped.

Remove the sweetbreads and keep warm, then carefully add the red currant jelly, vinegar, and warm beef stock to the pan, making sure that the oil doesn't spit. Increase the heat and boil fast, stirring until the sauce has reduced to half its volume. Meanwhile, toast the brioche slices.

When the sauce is nice and sticky, finish it off by adding the parsley and butter and stir through. Put a slice of brioche on each plate, top with sweetbreads, and pour the sauce on top.

Serve with a green salad or green beans tossed in butter.

TURDUCKEN

It's an awful name for an extraordinary dish. The name "turducken" is a combination of **tur**key, **duck,** and chi**cken**. (I've been trying to come up with a new name, but all I can think of is "turkchickuck," which is, let's face it, worse.) The dish is a poultry Russian doll, offering a chicken stuffed inside a duck, stuffed inside a turkey. Turducken is traditional Thanksgiving fare in Louisiana, but I usually make one at Christmas or for New Year's, when I go to town using as many different birds as I can. The most elaborate version I can boast is an eight-bird roast of turkey stuffed with goose, capon, chicken, guinea fowl, woodcock, quail, and pigeon breast—with a little chipolata inside.

The trick is to bone the birds entirely so that you have one large hunk of meat. You make up for the lack of crispy skin on the inner birds by including a layer of something else—I like to add thinly sliced fruit and herbs (although in Louisiana, they add a variety of stuffings)—then, when you cut it open, you get a jelly roll effect.

You can buy ready-boned and rolled turduckens all set for the oven, but I think that you might feel undeserving of the applause at the table. It's fun to do it all yourself, although there are a couple of slightly tricky stages that I'll point out now to avoid disappointment halfway through. When you bone the turkey, you need to cut the meat away from the bones very carefully so that the skin remains intact—at least over the main bulk of the breast, where it touches the breastbone—and this is sometimes difficult. This will take time, possibly an hour or more, depending on your knife skills, and it's best not to rush it. You'll need to sew up the whole turducken once you've rolled it up, and, although I've done this a few times with a sharp knife and some string, it's much easier to use a trussing needle (just a big needle, really) and butcher's twine, both of which are readily available in cookware stores or online. I should also point out that this is a slow-cooked dish, which will need several hours in the oven. Don't let that put you off, though!

SERVES ABOUT 14–16

11lb turkey
5½lb duck
2½lb chicken
salt and freshly ground black pepper
fresh thyme leaves
2 oranges, peeled and thinly sliced
2 lemons, peeled and thinly sliced
olive oil
a splash of white wine

Bone all the birds, taking your time so that you don't cut through the skin accidentally. Using a sharp, thin knife, cut the skin along the backbone first, then ease the skin away from the chest cavity using lots of little cuts, following the bones until you get to the legs, then cut into the meat and separate the socket from the main carcass. Leave the leg bones in for the moment, and concentrate on cutting the meat away from the carcass, continuing with little cuts. Be very careful at the top of the breast, where the skin is all that keeps it together—here, you must be careful not to slice the skin. Now, do the other side.

Boning the legs is a bit tricky (you can leave them in if you don't feel confident): you'll need to scrape the flesh away from the bone bit by bit, working your way down and turning it inside out until you get to the end. Push the meat back into the skin. Unless you're really in the groove of it, I suggest that you chop off the drumsticks and wings if they

are simply too much effort. (This will obviously leave a little slit in the skin, but it's not a problem.) Continue until you've boned all three birds.

Preheat the oven to 350°F. Now, place the turkey skin-side down, season with salt and pepper, sprinkle a few thyme leaves over the top and lay some orange and lemon slices on the meat. Place the duck on top of that and repeat the layer of seasoning, thyme, and orange and lemon slices; then place the chicken on top. Add a couple of orange and lemon slices in the middle.

Now, you need to truss the stuffed birds into as neat a roll as you can. This is best done by rolling up the birds and sewing up the turkey using a trussing needle and twine. Unless you really want to keep it as a surprise, I'd suggest that you enlist the help of a friend at this stage.

Brush the turducken with olive oil and season with salt and pepper, then carefully massage the oil into the skin (this will help to stop the skin from splitting). Place the turducken, breast-side down, in a roasting pan, add a splash of white wine, then cover it with foil. Roast for about 2 ½ hours, basting every 30 minutes or so (this helps to keep the skin from splitting, which can sometimes happen), and each time removing and reserving all but a few tablespoons of excess juices, (often, there is a *lot* of juice!) Remove the foil and roast for another 30 minutes. Check that the turducken is cooked by inserting a knife into a thick part of it—the juices should run clear. Cook for a little longer, if need be, but be careful not to overcook it, or it will be very dry.

Remove the turducken from the oven. Re-cover it with foil and leave it in the pan with some of the juices to rest for 30 minutes while you make some gravy. Put the reserved cooking juices in a saucepan and reduce by half, adding a little flour to thicken, if you prefer thick gravy.

Carve, giving each person a section through the birds.

Serve with roasted potatoes, roasted parsnips, buttered carrots, buttered cabbage or greens, gravy, and cranberry sauce.

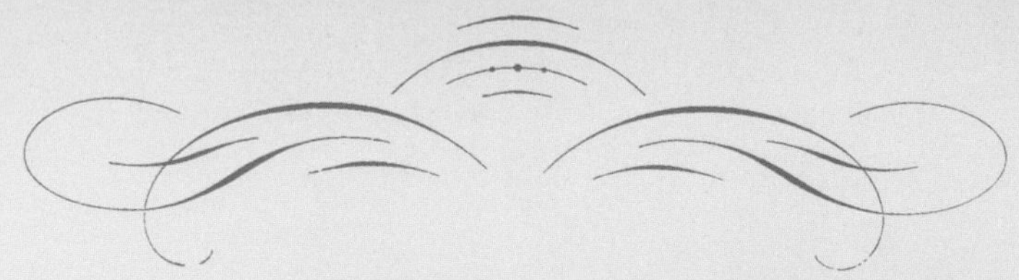

CHOCOLATE-ROASTED SPARE RIBS

I once saw a man—I kid you not—eating spare ribs with a knife and fork. I nearly asked him if he was paying penance for some unspeakable sin, but then I remembered that there's a generation for whom touching food with fingers is simply out of the question. Thankfully, those days are over, and we can now revel in the laying on of hands. Ribs (and rib sauce fingers) were made for slurping, licking, sucking, and generally slobbering over, and these chocolatey ones make them almost unbearably delicious. Just leave the cutlery in the drawer.

This chocolate marinade gives the ribs a rich, smoky flavor that everyone seems to love. You might be tempted to use more chocolate than the recipe suggests, but resist! Too much will make this dish cloying.

SERVES 6

3½lb pork ribs, skin removed, cut into separate ribs

FOR THE MARINADE
½ cup tomato paste
4oz dark chocolate, grated
1 mild red chile, finely chopped (or 1 teaspoon red chile flakes)
1¼in thumb of ginger, peeled and grated
1 teaspoon Chinese five-spice powder (optional)
2 tablespoons vegetable oil
2 tablespoons honey
salt and freshly ground black pepper

Preheat the oven to 400°F (or better still, start up your barbecue). Place all the marinade ingredients into a saucepan and simmer over medium heat for 2 minutes, stirring to prevent the marinade from burning.

Lay the ribs in one or two roasting pans, not too tightly packed (they can sometimes release a fair amount of moisture and you want them to roast, not poach; if they poach, they can turn out a little rubbery).

Pour the sauce over the top and stir to make sure that the ribs are thoroughly coated. Roast uncovered in the oven for about 20–30 minutes, turning once. Check that the ribs are cooked through, then serve with rice and sesame stir-fried cabbage.

Lindt

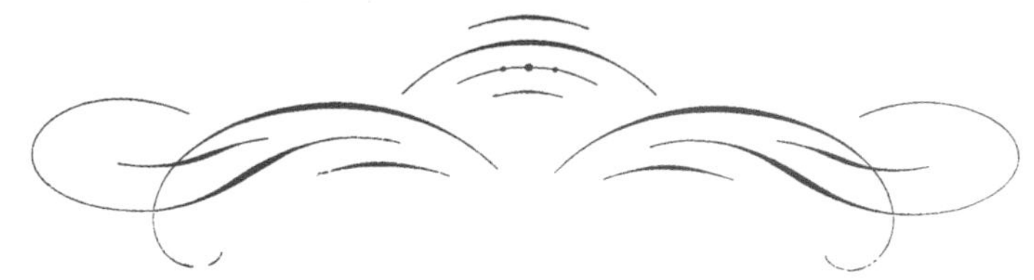

BRAISED LAMBS' HEARTS WITH GREMOLATA

Simple, delicious, and oh-so-cheap, this slow-cooked dish tastes, oddly enough, like a very tender beef stew and has the texture of beef tenderloin. Six lambs' hearts cost less than my Sunday newspaper, so it's strange they aren't eaten more often. The idea of eating hearts may be off-putting to some, but these are so good that if any dish were to convince you to eat more offal, this should be the one.

Of course, gremolata spreads a little joy over anything it touches—it's an amazing Italian mixture of herbs, garlic, and lemon zest, which, added to any stew after it's been cooked, turns a simple, hearty dish into an explosion of flavor.

SERVES 6

6 lambs' hearts
2 tablespoons all-purpose flour
3 tablespoons vegetable or non-virgin olive oil
1¾lb root vegetables (e.g., a mixture of parsnips, carrots, and Jerusalem artichokes), chopped into large chunks
salt and freshly ground black pepper
1¼ cup red wine
1 cup good chicken stock
14oz baby new potatoes (peeled or not—it's up to you)
8 garlic cloves, roughly chopped
4 bay leaves
bouquet garni of parsley and thyme stems tied together with string

FOR THE GREMOLATA
grated zest of 2 lemons
2 tablespoons lemon juice
3 garlic cloves, finely chopped
a handful of finely chopped fresh thyme, rosemary, and parsley

The hearts need little preparation; simply cut out the tube/ventricle ends, which descend an inch or so into the top of the heart. Don't worry about making a neat job of it and don't cut off the little layers of fat that sit around the top—it's fabulous stuff and helps to moisten the dish.

Spread out the flour on a plate and roll the hearts around in it to coat them thoroughly. Take a heavy-bottomed casserole dish (or any good pan with a lid), add the oil, and brown the hearts in two batches over high heat for about 6–8 minutes, turning to sear them all around. Remove the hearts and set aside, then add the root vegetables (but not the potatoes) to the pan and fry for 10 minutes.

Season with salt and pepper and add the wine, stock, potatoes, garlic, bay leaves, and bouquet garni to the pan. Increase the heat until the liquid starts to simmer, then put the lid on the pan and reduce the heat to as low as possible, using a heat diffuser if you have one, so that the liquid just simmers gently. Simmer for 2–4 hours (you can also do this in the oven set to 225°F, if you prefer), checking every now and then to make sure it isn't drying out and adding water, if necessary.

Meanwhile, make the gremolata by stirring together the lemon zest and juice, garlic, and herbs in a bowl. Set aside.

Uncover the pan and remove and discard the bouquet garni. Using a slotted spoon, decant the meat and vegetables to a large bowl, leaving all the juices behind. Boil the juices for about 5–10 minutes, or until they have reduced to a good thick gravy. Serve the hearts, vegetables, and gravy in wide bowls, scattering the gremolata over each one just before serving.

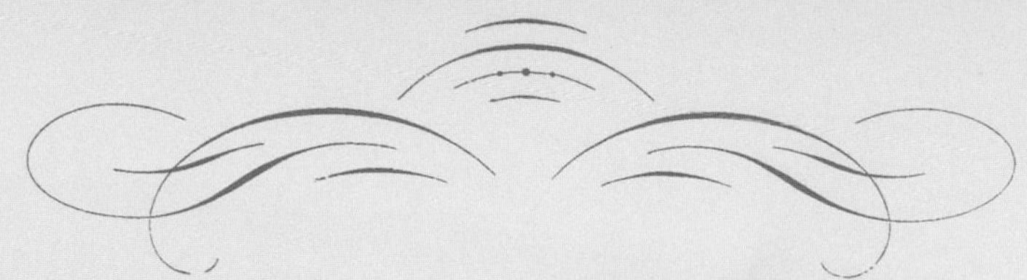

ORANGE AND GARLIC-CRUSTED LEG OF LAMB

Leg of lamb is so lean that it works beautifully with this spectacular cooking method. Basically, you encase the meat in a thick layer of oranges, rosemary, and thyme, so that the lamb gets the benefits of both roasting and steaming but doesn't dry out. The resulting meat has a wonderfully fragrant, herbal taste, and although the color of the oranges fades a little during cooking, the dish still looks spectacular when it arrives on the table. I've also made this dish a few times with a lemon crust, which works well, as do satsumas (especially good around Christmas). Spanish blood oranges are particularly good to use when they are in season, because of their intense flavor and color. Steer clear of navel oranges, however, since they have too much pith.

SERVES 8

1 leg of lamb

FOR THE CRUST
4 oranges, chopped into chunks
8 large garlic cloves, peeled and roughly chopped
3 tablespoons fresh rosemary leaves
2 tablespoons fresh thyme leaves
1 teaspoon salt

FOR THE GRAVY
¾ cup white wine
¾ cup chicken stock
juice of ¼ orange

Remove the leg of lamb from the fridge and set aside to return to room temperature. Preheat the oven to 400°F. Combine all the crust ingredients in a food processor and process until the mixture has the texture of hummus. Spread a small pool of the paste on the base of a large roasting pan and place the lamb on top of it. Now, spread the rest of the paste all over the lamb until it's completely covered. Cover loosely with foil and roast for 1½ hours (or longer, if you like your lamb well done).

Now, for the gravy: Pour the wine and stock into a saucepan and simmer for 10 minutes, then add the orange juice. Finally, turn the heat off and cover with a lid to keep warm.

When the lamb is cooked, take it out of the roasting pan, place on a board, and cover with foil to rest for 30 minutes. Scrape most of the crust out of the roasting pan, reserving a couple of ladelfuls to use for the gravy. (Don't use burned or blackened pieces, though, since these will make the gravy taste bitter.) Add the wine, chicken stock, and orange gravy to the pan and place over low heat. Stir the reserved crust mixture into the stock a spoonful at a time, tasting each time you add, until you have a good, fragrant gravy. Strain before serving.

After the lamb has rested for at least 30 minutes, carve it at the table and serve with gravy, green beans, and roasted potatoes.

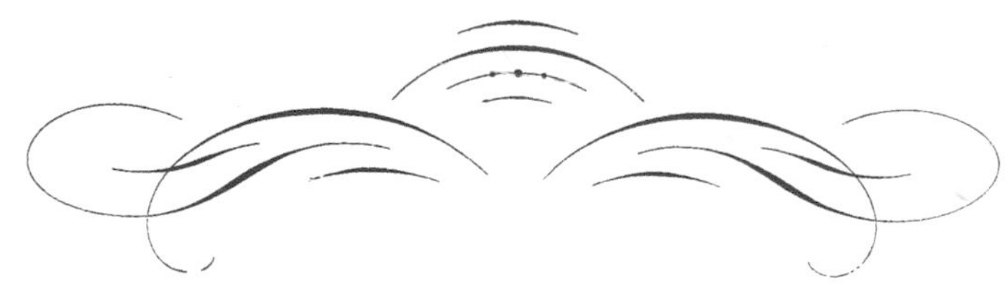

TAGINE OF LAMB WITH APRICOTS AND PRUNES

You don't need a real tagine to make this Moroccan classic—a casserole dish with a good lid will do—but there is a certain spectacle to be had from placing this extraordinary clay witch's hat on the table. If you have your own clay tagine, yes, you are supposed to put it directly on the heat on your stove, although it feels uncomfortable to do so.

I should add that, although this dish needs a few hours of cooking time, it's not one of those slow-cooked dishes for which you can use cheap cuts of lamb like shanks—you really need to use leg or trimmed shoulder meat.

SERVES 6

2¼lb diced leg of lamb, or lamb shoulder, trimmed of most of the fat
¼ cup olive oil
1 large onion, finely chopped
4 large garlic cloves, finely chopped
2 cinnamon sticks, or 1 teaspoon ground cinnamon
1 teaspoon ground coriander
1 teaspoon ground cumin
1 x 15oz can chickpeas, drained
1 x 14½oz can chopped plum tomatoes
1½ cups chicken stock
1in piece fresh ginger, grated
9oz dried apricots and/or prunes
1 strip orange peel
18oz butternut squash, peeled and cut into chunks
a bunch of cilantro, finely chopped (stems chopped and reserved)

Heat 2 tablespoons olive oil in a casserole dish or tagine, then brown the lamb, a batch at a time, over high heat. Remove the lamb and set aside.

Reduce the heat, add the onion, and fry until soft and browned. Stir in the garlic, cinnamon, ground coriander, and cumin, and fry for 1 minute, then add the chickpeas, tomatoes, chicken stock, ginger, and dried fruit. Stir, bring to a simmer, then cover and simmer very gently for 1½ hours. Add the orange peel, butternut squash, and the cilantro stems. Simmer very gently for another 30 minutes.

Meanwhile, prepare the couscous. In a heatproof bowl, pour boiling water over the couscous until it's covered (use good-quality stock, if you prefer). Cover and leave to soak for 15 minutes, then check that the couscous is tender (add a few tablespoons more boiling water if not and leave to rest for another 5 minutes). Stir in the chopped cilantro leaves and 2 tablespoons of olive oil and season to taste.

Serve the tagine with couscous and some harissa, for your friends to add as they wish.

7 DESSERTS

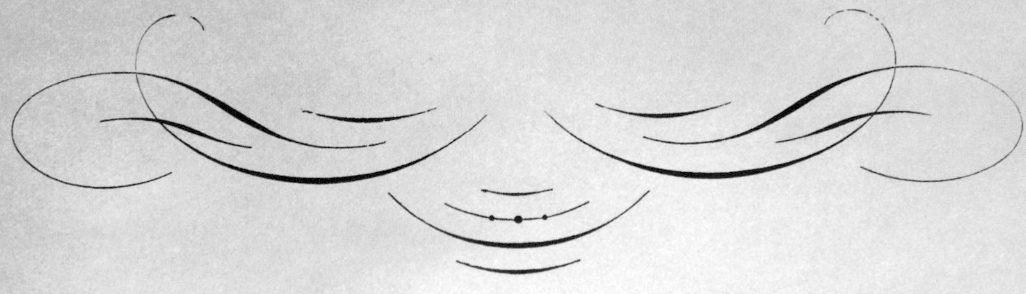

THE RECIPES HERE ARE MOSTLY SIMPLE and easily achievable to the extent of laziness. For instance, there's really nothing more to Bowls of Candy than some candies and a bowl to put them in. I couldn't resist giving you a recipe for liquid nitrogen-made ice cream—even though I'm aware that you may not have access to the stuff—but, for the most part, these are intriguing but incredibly simple desserts, which is the way I think desserts should be. My friends are always over the moon to get anything at the end of a meal (or are too full to contemplate another mouthful), so they are invariably happy with whatever I rustle up. Our family favorite is Pop Rock-Encrusted Pineapple Carpaccio, which is much easier than it sounds to make, yet it's a riotous combination of flavor and physical sensations.

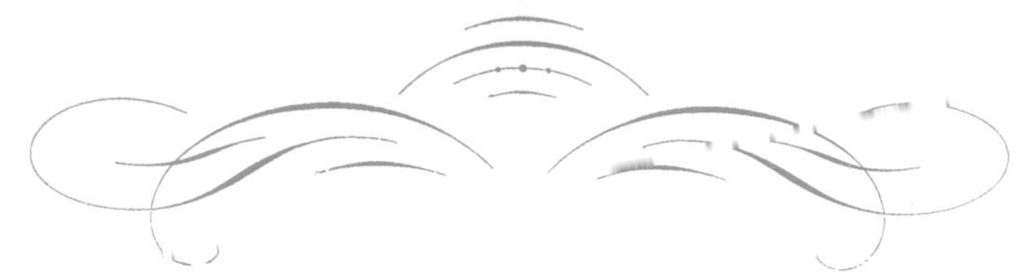

APPLE BOBBING

Apples have attracted an extraordinary amount of myth and legend since day one (if the Old Testament is anything to go by), with Eve getting us all kicked out of the Garden of Eden in Genesis 1–5. One apple, and we were cursed with mortality, hard labor, and tortures like reality television. (Or was that a bit later?) Anyway, it may interest you to know that the very first apples were pretty grim: tiny, sour little fruits that tasted like crabapples in a bad mood. They were also one of the first fruits ever to have been cultivated, so it's no surprise that they have attracted a lot of attention.

Bobbing is my favorite apple-based diversion (alongside wassailing, which involves drinking a hard cider punch and singing songs so ancient that nobody notices that you're drunk or wildly out of tune, or both). Apple bobbing originates from Celtic times, when apples were linked with fertility. There's a fair amount of bawdiness surrounding a lot of the myths, but, since this is a family-friendly book, we'll stick with the lovely one that if a girl manages to bob an apple and puts it under her pillow, she will dream of her future lover.

The basic principles of apple bobbing are as follows:

- Fill a large, clean bucket with fresh drinkable water, then add a couple dozen small apples. The apples are less dense than the water, so they float.
- Give players a certain amount of time (let's say one minute) to pick up as many apples as they can manage using only their teeth, and (if they can't be trusted) with hands held behind their backs.
- Don't tell anyone, but the trick is to push your head and face into the water (you will, of course, get soaking wet) and trap the apple against the side of the bucket. You'll then be able to sink your teeth into it and pull it out.

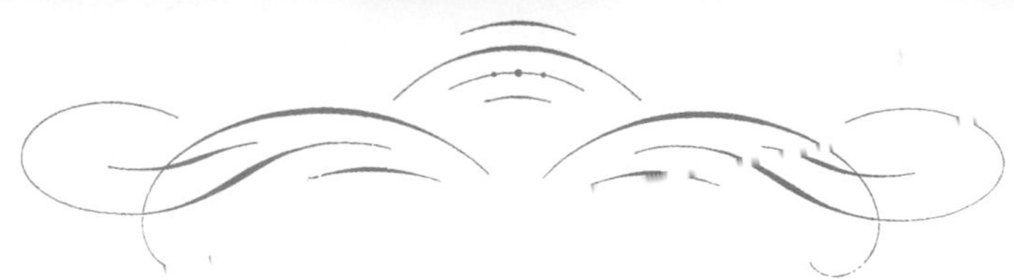

MANGO HEDGEHOGS

I'll never forget the experience of eating ripe mangoes straight from the tree in Haiti. I didn't need to bother peeling them, since the skins were still pretty thin—I just wiped them down a bit and then sank my teeth in and ripped out a chunk of the juicy flesh. The heady, sweet, fragrant flavors shot into my nose and made me gasp with pleasure. If only Haiti could find a way to export more of them, perhaps it would help the country claw its way out of poverty. The nearest I've ever found to those flavor explosions are the yellow Indian Alphonso mangoes, which have only in the last few years become available in the United States—at long last.

Mango-eating styles vary wildly from person to person. I prefer to eat my mangoes with my wife in the bathtub, but if she's not available, this hedgehog technique works just as well at the table. All you do is cut the mango and then turn it inside out. Then you can either get your face deep into it, or slice individual cubes off using a knife.

First, cut the mango into three segments using a sharp knife, cutting around the long flat pit in the middle and leaving it in a central segment. Hold the mango up on its edge and slice down off-center, carving around the pit (which will be about 1in thick at the widest point). Do the same on the other side of the mango. Make crosshatched cuts into the flesh, cutting up to, but not through, the skin; then turn the mango inside out. Serve with a lime segment for squeezing on top for extra zing.

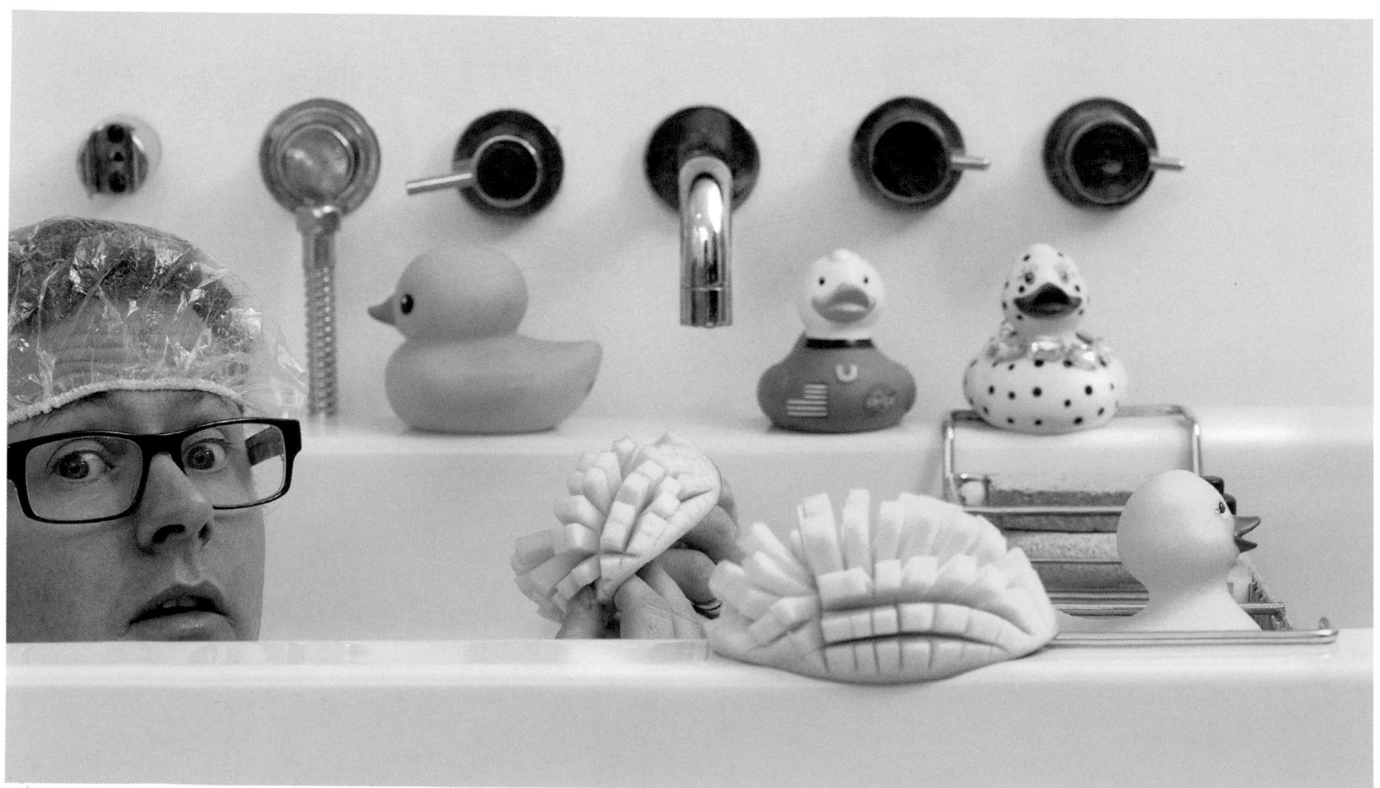

ICE POPS

I'm not sure if it's really fair to call this a recipe, since all that I'm suggesting you do is take some of your favorite juices and fruits and freeze them. I guess the only reason I'm telling you about ice pops is to remind myself how nice they are to share on a hot day, so that I remember to make them in advance. I've made some complicated and inventive versions in the past—jellyfish and elder flower were particularly fun—but I think it's just as good to stick with what you love.

You can make ice pops using your own plastic cups and some popsicle sticks, but the easiest method is to buy some ice pop molds. Fill them with whatever's on hand: orange juice, elder flower cordial (with some flowers thrown in, too, if it's the season), perhaps some strawberry or cranberry juice. One little physics-based note of advice: the faster your ice pops freeze, the fewer large ice crystals will form in them, and the better they will be.

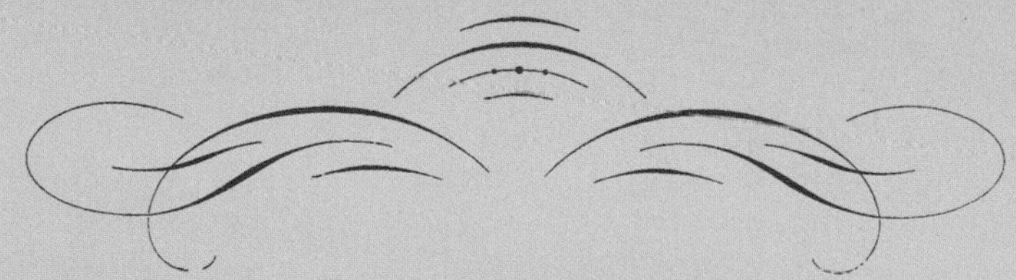

CHOCOLATE FRUITFEST

There's nothing more to these than fruit dipped into melted chocolate, yet when I serve them to my friends they always go a little bit crazy. These are also a very sneaky way to get picky kids to eat fresh fruit (and if you use good dark chocolate, you can even claim that they're healthy). Don't worry if you don't have any parchment paper—you can make these on any nonstick surface, such as a baking sheet or frying pan.

SERVES 6

1½lb assorted fruit: grapes, strawberries, cherries, blueberries, raspberries, or fig slices
4oz good-quality dark chocolate, broken into chunks

Wash and prepare your fruit: Pull the grapes off the stem but leave cherry and strawberry stems on, then lay the fruit on some paper towels to dry and put in the fridge to chill.

Melt the chocolate in a heatproof bowl over a saucepan of barely simmering water. Stir it just until it melts (you don't want to heat it any more than necessary), then remove from the heat.

Lay some parchment paper on a baking sheet that will fit in your fridge. Dip the chilled fruit into the melted chocolate and lay on the paper. Store in the fridge until you're ready to serve.

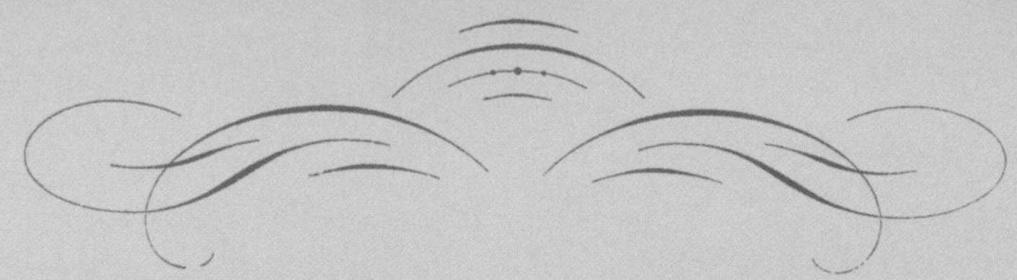

POP-ROCK-ENCRUSTED PINEAPPLE CARPACCIO

You may know Pop Rocks as popping candy, Space Dust, Space Rocks, or perhaps Fizz Wiz. It's a sugary candy that comes in tiny packages containing a teaspoonful or so of sugary crumbs that crackle and pop when they dissolve in your mouth. You can actually hear and feel the little pops on your tongue, and it's lots of fun. The candy is made by cooking sugar syrup together with carbon dioxide and then chilling it under pressure to set little pressurized bubbles inside the candy. When it dissolves in your mouth, these bubbles are released with a "pop."

Pop Rocks were invented in 1956 by chemist William Mitchell while he was working for the General Foods Corporation. It's a bit of a retro candy these days, but you can still buy it (see Suppliers, page 218) and it's great to use as a frosting for your margarita glasses instead of salt and to add to desserts like this one. You need to add it at the last minute to anything that isn't too dry, otherwise it will dissolve and pop before your friends get to eat it.

My tip with this dish is not to tell your friends what's in it until the Pop Rocks start popping in their mouths!

SERVES 6

1 large pineapple, peeled and cored
2 tablespoons mint leaves, finely chopped
6 tablespoons Greek yogurt
1 tablespoon honey
2 tablespoons confectioners' sugar
2 x ⅓oz packages Pop Rocks

Slice the pineapple as thinly as you can, and divide it up between six individual plates, laying the slices out so they overlap. In a small bowl, combine half the mint leaves, the Greek yogurt, and honey and mix thoroughly. Put a dollop of this in the middle of each plate, then put the confectioners' sugar in a strainer and lightly dust each plate with it. Sprinkle on the Pop Rocks and then scatter the remaining mint leaves on top.

NET WT 5g

TOFFEE APPLES

Go on, do it for the kids! To avoid disappointment, bear in mind that your sugar *must* reach hard crack stage, otherwise you'll be left with a sloppy, sticky mess that's a nightmare to deal with. You'll need a clean, sturdy twig or popsicle stick for each toffee apple.

MAKES 10 TOFFEE APPLES

10 small apples, preferably Cox's Orange Pippin
3¾ cups demerara sugar
1 tablespoon vinegar
2 tablespoons golden syrup (or 1 tablespoon honey and 1 tablespoon light corn syrup)
½ cup butter
butter, for greasing

Wash and rub dry your apples with a cloth so that you remove any wax from the surface (this can stop the toffee from sticking). Wash your twigs or sticks, too, for good measure. Cut the bottoms of the twigs at an angle so that they're sharp, then firmly impale the apples with them.

Put the sugar and ¾ cup water in a heavy-bottomed pan over medium heat. Stir until the sugar has dissolved, then stir in the vinegar, golden syrup, and butter, until melted. Bring to a boil and continue to boil vigorously for about 30–45 minutes. It needs to reach "hard crack" stage (that's around 300°F, in case you have a candy thermometer), otherwise it won't set hard. Test the toffee after 30 minutes by dropping a spoonful of it into a pan of cold water—it's ready if it hardens in the water. If it remains sticky, continue to boil, then test again.

Lay some parchment paper on a board or tray and lightly grease it with butter. Dip the apples into the toffee, twisting them around until they are well coated. Turn each one gently 10–12 times as the toffee begins to harden, then place on the parchment paper and leave to set.

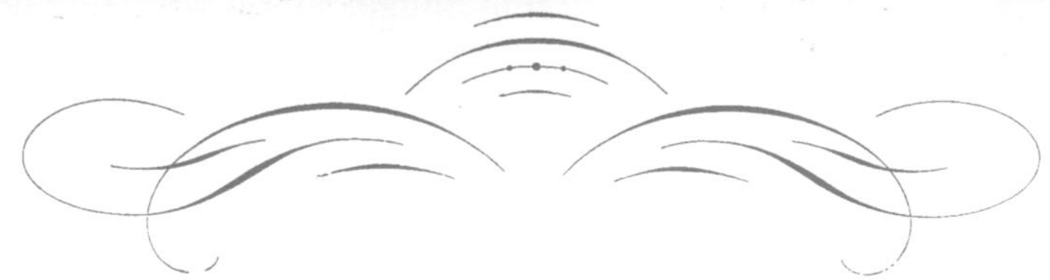

FLUORESCENT JELLO

This isn't a cheat, and it's not an optical illusion—these are simply gin and tonic jellos made by adding gelatin to G&T and leaving them to set. So why are they glowing that fantastic ghostly color? The answer is that quinine (the bitter flavoring in tonic water) glows under UV fluorescent light. If you want to serve this to kids or teetotallers, it works just as well without the gin.

The great thing about G&T jello (other than its glowiness) is that you can serve it either before the meal as a solid G&T, complete with its bubbles captured in the gelatin (yes, the picture below really does show a G&T with trapped bubbles, and the gelatin even retains a little fizz), or you can have them after your meal as a wonderfully crazy dessert. Either way, it's best to place them all on the table without drawing attention to them, and then switch on your fluorescent bulb and place it as close to the jellos as is safe before you switch off the lights.

Just buy a UV fluorescent light (easily found at hardware stores or on the web) and you're off. The bigger the bulb, the better the glow. I should add that the inspiration for these jellos comes from my crazy chemist friend Dr. Andrea Sella and the equally crazy Bompass & Parr, self-described jellymongers to the great and the good, who kindly showed me and some fascinated kids how to make a fluorescent St. Paul's Cathedral for my *Gastronuts* TV show.

MAKES 2 QUARTS (ENOUGH FOR 8 HIGHBALL GLASSES OR 3–4 GELATIN MOLDS)

- 2 packages of sheet gelatin (enough to set 2 quarts firmly—usually about 50 percent more than listed on the package)
- 2 cups good-quality gin (you can substitute extra tonic for the gin if you don't want to serve alcohol)
- juice of 3 large lemons
- 1 ½ quarts tonic water (chilled before use, if possible)
- 8 lemon slices, to garnish (optional)

Cut the gelatin sheets into small pieces using scissors and put them into a large heatproof bowl. Pour 1 cup of gin over the gelatin and leave for 10 minutes so the gelatin starts to soften. Put the bowl in a microwave and heat on high power for 1 ½ minutes (or place the bowl over a saucepan of boiling water), then stir until the gelatin has completely dissolved. Don't let it boil.

Stir the remaining gin and the lemon juice into the gelatin, then add the chilled tonic water, pouring it in as carefully as you can to keep it from fizzing (you want to lock in all those bubbles).

If you are using gelatin molds, lightly grease them inside using vegetable oil on a piece of paper towels. Pour the G&T mixture, equally carefully, into your gelatin molds or glasses, garnish with lemon slices, if using, and place in the fridge to set for about 6 hours.

Serve under UV light. The darker it is, the better the effect, so serve at night, with the lights turned out and the UV bulb as close to the jellos as possible!

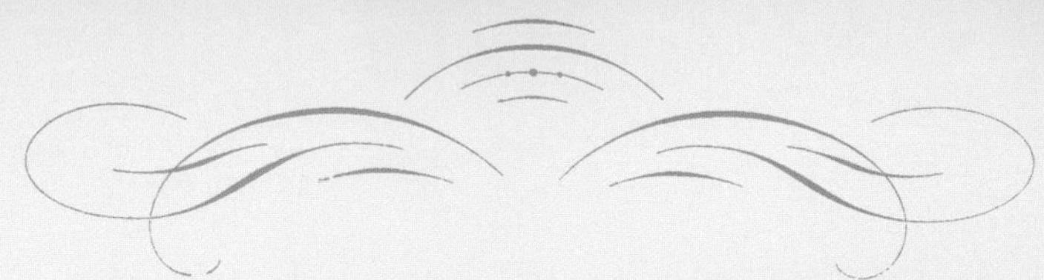

LIQUID NITROGEN AND LEMONGRASS ICE CREAM

Liquid nitrogen boils at –321°F, which really is very cold indeed. On the one hand, this makes it lots of fun to play with, since you can pour it directly into a substance that you want to chill, releasing plumes of mist, delighting the kids and scaring the cat. On the other hand, its instability—and the danger that it will freeze your hand so cold that it will snap off—means that liquid nitrogen can be hard to find at the mall. Fortunately for me, my great chemist friend, Dr. Sella, has a good supply of the stuff, and, for a contribution to the school Petri-dish fund, he will let me have some.

One very strange fact about liquid nitrogen is that it's an incredibly cheap substance. The downside is that you need some very expensive high-tech storage facilities to keep it at home, and special double-walled vacuum flasks to transport it in. Liquid nitrogen is distilled from liquid air (air that has been compressed and cooled to temperatures so low that it condenses to a liquid), and since our atmosphere is 78 percent nitrogen (and 21 percent oxygen), there's a lot of it around. It's perfectly safe to pour liquid nitrogen into your food as long as it's not too cold to bear—it all boils away as soon as it warms above -321°F and, in any case, we breath the stuff all the time. It's even used in some food-production processes, for instance, mayonnaise-making, to cool food quickly so that bacteria are less likely to multiply in it. Weird, huh?

Dr. Sella loves playing with this stuff (he dips his finger in it, which is apparently fine as long as you take it right out), and I've even seen him pouring it in his mouth and spitting it out to make instant snow. If you ever manage to get your hands on some liquid nitrogen, *do not try this at home*—Andrea can do this because he is a chemist and entirely bonkers.

This recipe is actually a very delicious and practical one that you can make with or without liquid nitrogen—for instance, with an ice-cream maker. The original version had jellyfish in it, but what with one thing and another, that seemed like overkill.

SERVES 6

3 lemongrass stems, outer skin peeled off, insides finely chopped
¾ cup heavy cream
¾ cup coconut milk
⅔ cup whole milk
4 eggs, yolks only
½ cup superfine sugar
zest of 1 lime
liquid nitrogen

Put the first four ingredients in a saucepan. Bring to a boil over medium heat, then remove the pan from the heat and leave to cool for 5 minutes. Meanwhile, in a separate bowl, beat the egg yolks, sugar, and lime zest until pale. Place the pan of lemongrass mixture over low heat, and add the egg and sugar mixture. Heat gently, stirring all the time, until the mixture thickens slightly to form a light custard. Don't let it boil or overheat, otherwise the eggs will curdle. Strain out the lemongrass.

If you have an ice-cream maker, use it to make the ice cream. Otherwise, put your safety goggles on and carefully stir in the liquid nitrogen a splash at a time, letting each splash boil off before you add the next one, until the ice cream freezes. Warning: If you pour in too much nitrogen at once, you are likely to create superchilled lumps rather than a nice, smooth, edible mixture. Don't turn the ice cream solid, or it will be too cold to eat.

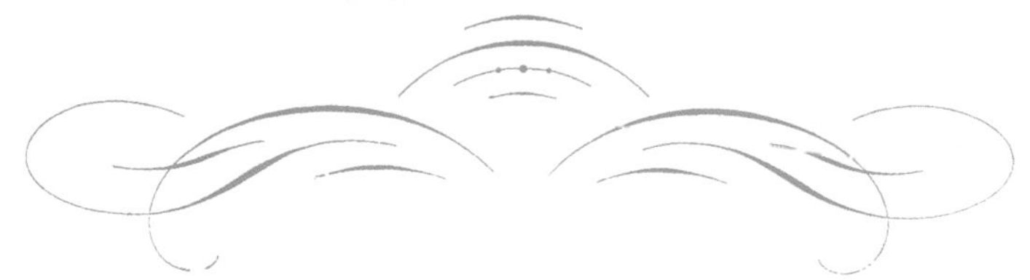

LIMONCELLO FRUIT JELLOFEST

These are ridiculously easy to make. You *could* create your own homemade flavors from gelatin-based concoctions, but if you're going to do that, I'd save the effort for making the fluorescent G&T jellos on page 194, or for flights of elder flower-based fancy when the season is right (when spring is about to tumble into summer). No, for these, I'd just use good-quality concentrated lemon gelatin, adding a sour kick of lemon juice to balance the sweetness, and a good dose of limoncello (a delicious lemon liqueur). If you don't have any limoncello, vodka is a pretty good substitute. (For committed jelloboozers, here's a fascinating article on how much alcohol you can add to gelatin before it refuses to set: http://www.myscienceproject.org/j-shot.html). If you're serving the jellos to kids, you should obviously leave out the booze.

SERVES 6

1 package of good-quality concentrated lemon gelatin
juice of ½ lemon
⅔ cup limoncello or vodka
assorted fruit (but not figs or pineapple, which stop the gelatin from setting)

Make the gelatin according to the instructions on the package, but use only half the quantity of water called for, to allow for the lemon juice and spirits. Add the lemon juice and limoncello or vodka and stir in. Divide the fruit between small glasses and pour over the gelatin mixture. Place the jellos in the fridge and leave to set for at least 4 hours.

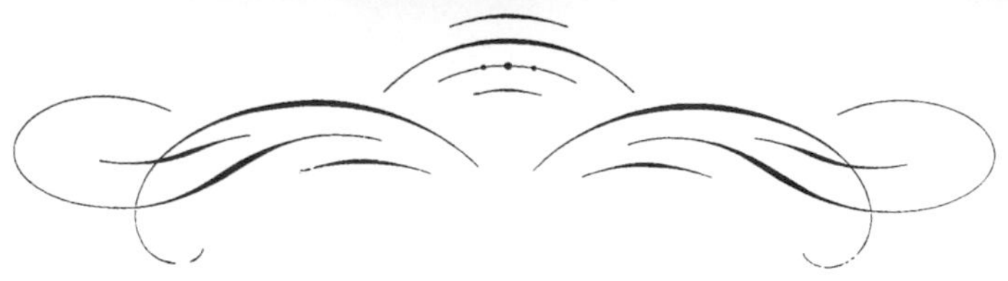

MERINGUES

There's a beautiful symmetry to the fact that my wife Georgia loves to cook two things more than anything else: hand-beaten mayonnaise (egg yolks) and meringues (egg whites). When either of these is on the menu, I retire gracefully from the kitchen until given the official all-clear.

Cooking times for meringues are heavily dependent on size. For dinky little ones, 15–20 minutes might suffice. For a pavlova-esque whopper, you could be looking at an hour. You need to keep an eye on them. Oh, and meringues seem to work best when the eggs *aren't* superfresh.

MAKES 24 SMALL MERINGUES OR 6 LARGE ONES

butter, for greasing
4 medium egg whites (save the yolks for the mayonnaise recipe on page 121)
2/3 cup superfine sugar
1 cup confectioners' sugar, sifted
½ teaspoon vanilla extract
1 teaspoon cornstarch
1 teaspoon white wine vinegar
optional toppings and flavorings: blueberries and/or raspberries, lightly crushed into a mush, candies, and cake decorations

Preheat the oven to 300°F. Lay parchment paper on a baking sheet and lightly grease with butter.

Combine the egg whites and superfine sugar in a bowl and whisk them until the mixture forms stiff peaks. Add the confectioners' sugar, vanilla extract, cornstarch, and vinegar and beat for another 5 minutes.

Spoon the mixture out onto the baking sheet in your chosen style, then, if you're using them, drop over a teaspoon of your chosen topping and gently mix it in.

Bake small meringues in the oven for about 20 minutes, checking them after 15 minutes, or large ones for about 40 minutes. You can test whether they are cooked by tapping them gently to check that they are solid; they shouldn't have turned brown. Remove from the oven and let cool before serving.

ETON MESS

SERVES 6

10oz ripe raspberries
¼ cup superfine sugar
7oz meringues (recipe at right)
¾ cup heavy cream, whipped until it forms soft peaks
7oz strawberries or mixed summer fruits, larger ones roughly chopped

First, make a raspberry sauce by laying a strainer on top of a bowl and pushing the berries through the strainer using the back of a spoon, catching the juice in the bowl. Stir the superfine sugar into the raspberry purée until it dissolves.

Break the meringue into rough hunks and place in a bowl, then fold the whipped cream and strawberries through it. Spoon the whole "mess" onto a large serving dish, then pour the raspberry sauce over the top and stir it throughout.

CHOCOLATE-COVERED CRUNCHY HONEYCOMB

I recently spent six days experimenting with honeycomb, malt, and chocolate combinations trying to recreate malted milk ball candies. Never before has so much effort and pain been expended for eight minutes of culinary telivision fluff. I nearly went crazy trying to get the balance right (although my rabid children reaped the benefits: "Hmm, not quite crispy enough, Daddy. Try again.").

The difficulty in malted-milk-ball-making lies not in the honeycomb-making. No, the trouble crops up when you add malt to the mixture, which messes with the delicate chemistry of sugar-setting, and as for trying to scoop perfect balls out of the mixture… suffice it to say, there's a good reason why candy companies have multimillion-dollar factories and teams of people who dedicate their lives to creating the perfect chocolatey snack. (If you're interested, they make perfect malty honeycomb balls by cooking them in a partial vacuum so that the bubbles develop just right, then coat them several times and spin them on rollers so that they set perfectly.) I'd just like to add that on the day of filming, my slightly gnarly-looking versions won 75 percent of the vote in a blind taste-test. I suspect the audience was being kind to me—they could tell by the feel of my bumpy versions which was which!

You can make all manner of fun shapes with the honeycomb, and you can also cover them in chocolate to make your own version of the honeycomb candy bar.

MAKES ALMOST 1 1/3 POUNDS

butter, for greasing
1 ¾ cups sugar
½ cup honey
2 tablespoons corn syrup
1 ½ teaspoons baking soda
18oz good-quality chocolate (dark or milk), broken into small chunks

Grease two large baking sheets with butter. Put the sugar, honey, corn syrup, and 1/3 cup water in a large saucepan and heat gently, stirring frequently with a wooden spoon until the sugar has dissolved entirely. Now turn the heat up to medium and let it boil. The mixture needs to reach the "hard crack" stage, which is around 300°F (if you have a candy thermometer), or when it turns a dark toffee color. This should take about 30 minutes.

Turn off the heat and quickly stir in the baking soda. The mixture will slowly start to foam up, and as it does so, pour half of it onto one baking sheet. On the other, try to make a series of dollops in fun shapes. (If it's too tricky, just make another big blob!). Leave the honeycomb to set for 2–3 hours — it needs to dry out thoroughly.

Break up the large blocks of solid honeycomb into chunks (a hammer or rolling pin may come in handy here). You could stop right here and eat it as it is, but if you want to go one step further you can cover it with chocolate to great effect.

Melt the chocolate in a heatproof bowl over a saucepan of barely simmering water. Stir the chocolate just until it melts (you don't want to heat it any more than necessary), then remove from the heat.

Lay some parchment paper on a tray (or a nonstick roasting pan) that will fit in your fridge. Dip each chunk of honeycomb into the chocolate and lay it on the parchment paper. Put in the fridge to set.

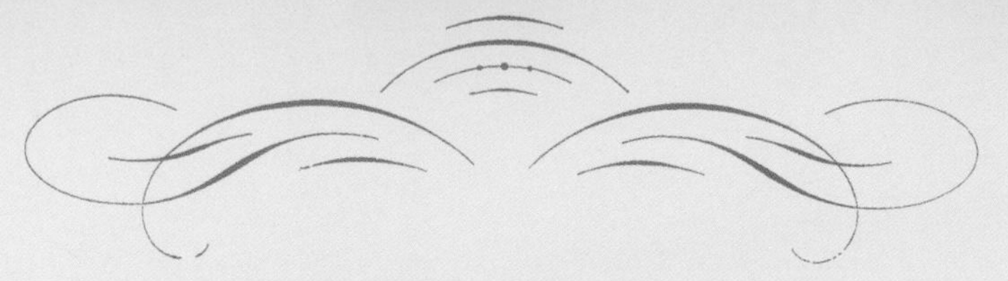

TOFFEE FONDUE

One of the great treats of my childhood was creeping downstairs in the early hours after my parents had had friends over for dinner. Their favorite dessert was a toffee fondue, and there was inevitably a pan of hardened toffee left on the table among the rest of the post-party wreckage. My sister Sam and I would gorge ourselves on the fudgey leftovers and marvel at the sophistication of it all.

This is a very rich dessert, but it's balanced by using cold, fresh fruit to dip into the toffee mixture. My favorite things to dip are cold grapes, taken straight from the fridge, which create an explosive combination of cold, firm crisp flesh inside a coating of hot, creamy gooey toffee.

You don't have to have a fondue set for this, although it does help. If you live in a fondue-free zone, just use the heaviest-bottomed saucepan you own and place it on the table on a cutting board so that it retains the heat for as long as possible (as the mixture cools, it gets stiffer, although it never really sets solid).

SERVES 8

¾lb chewy toffee candies
⅔ cup heavy cream

TO SERVE
2 apples, peeled, cored, cut into 1in squares
juice of ½ lemon
1lb grapes
½lb strawberries
4 satsumas

Refrigerate all the fruit you are going to use for dipping, tossing the apples in lemon juice to stop them from turning brown. Unwrap the toffees (it's essential that you use chewy, not crunchy, ones) and place them in a heavy-bottomed saucepan or fondue pan. Add the cream and place the pan over low heat, stirring gently until the toffees have melted and mixed in with the cream.

Just before you are ready to serve the fondue, remove the fruit from the fridge and divide the satsumas into segments. Put the fruit onto plates on the table and place the toffee mixture in the center. Give everyone a fork, fondue prong, or skewer so they can skewer the chilled fruit and then dunk it in the fondue. (Remember to leave behind a little pool of the toffee for your kids to wolf down in the morning!)

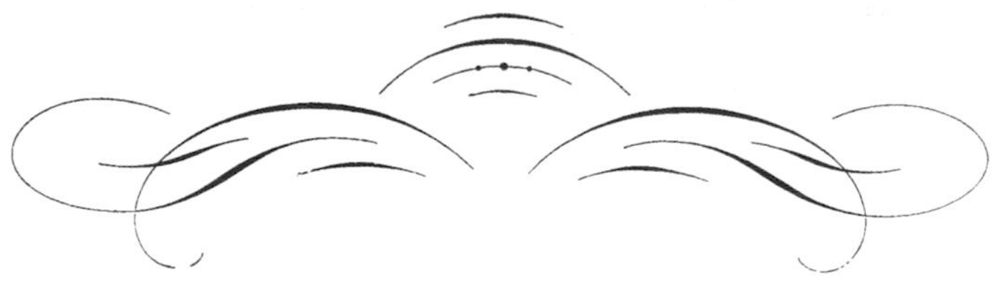

AFFOGATO

Never has so much culinary wonder come from so little effort. Affogato is a Milanese specialty that involves pouring a strong little espresso over a ball of vanilla ice cream. And that's it. You do, of course, need the means to make espresso, but beyond that, there's nothing to it.

SERVES 4

18oz good-quality vanilla ice cream
4 shots good, hot espresso

Place four glasses in the freezer to chill them a little (skip this bit if you're too hungry to wait), and when they're frosty, put a scoop of vanilla ice cream in each of them. Pour a shot of espresso over the top of each one and serve, with some amaretti cookies, if available (see page 206).

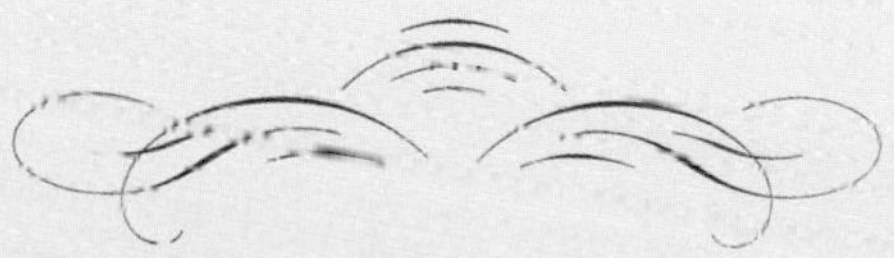

BOWLS OF CANDY

It's got to be the laziest dessert on the planet, but when you fill a few bowls with chocolates and candies and plonk them on the table after a big meal, everyone's eyes light up with childish pleasure. We all love a sophisticated fine pastry or refined fondant or coulis every now and then, but there's an extraordinarily joyous release when you indulge simpler pleasures. You'll wonder why you don't do it more often.

The only advice I can give is that the more childish or nostalgic the candies, the more your friends will love them. So let's hear it for Jelly Bellies, Gummi Bears, Sugar Babies, and Whoppers. (The latter are particularly good when melted into a coffee!)

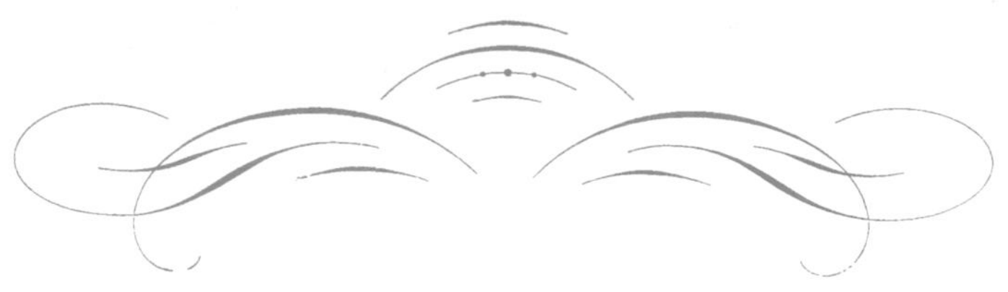

AMARETTI FUN

Amaretti are light almond cookies that are very nice to eat at the end of a meal with your coffee. But it's not so much their flavor that excites me as their packaging and the fun you can have with it. They usually arrive in pretty tins or boxes, but crucially, each cookie also comes wrapped in an extraordinary tissue paper that is extremely light and yet has enough structure to enable it to stand up on its own if rolled. This means that if you flatten out a wrapper then roll it up, you can set fire to it so that it burns down to the bottom and then flies up into the air.

When I first started doing this many years ago, the paper could be held in your hand and lit. If you were brave enough, it would lift up just before it scorched your hand. But the manufacturers seem to have changed their packaging material, and there's now no way you can do this without rolling up the wrapper and carefully laying it on a plate before lighting it.

Here's what you do. First, locate your fire extinguisher in case it all goes horribly wrong, then unwrap your amaretti and flatten the piece of paper out on the table. Next, roll it, stand it up on its end on a plate, and set fire to the top of it with a match. Sit back and keep a wary eye on it: The paper should burn down to the bottom and then, just when you're beginning to think it hasn't worked, it should lift up into the air—often by a few feet or so. Keep an eye out in case the embers don't go out and the burning wrapper sets fire to something.

WARNING: Only do this if you have a fire extinguisher on hand and, of course, please don't encourage your kids to play with fire!

DRINKS

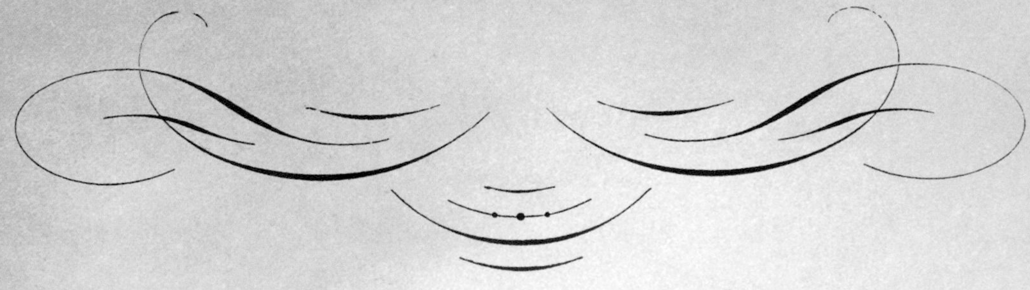

EXTRAORDINARY DRINKS are the icing on the cake of any extraordinary feast. You don't have to make them, but some of these are so simple, it seems rude not to, especially the fresh herbal teas that are an easy, yet sensuous and intriguing way to end a feast. And if you want to turn your dinner into a wild party, I offer you this one word of advice: cocktails. In my experience, any evening that starts with margarita invariably ends in riot. One cocktail sprinkles a little magic over dinner, and five cocktails generally means that you could serve grilled cheese sandwiches and still have a wild time. Just don't drink so many that you don't remember the meal the following day. That way lies madness, and, anyway, the whole point is to make a meal that everyone will remember forever. *Bon chance, mon brave.*

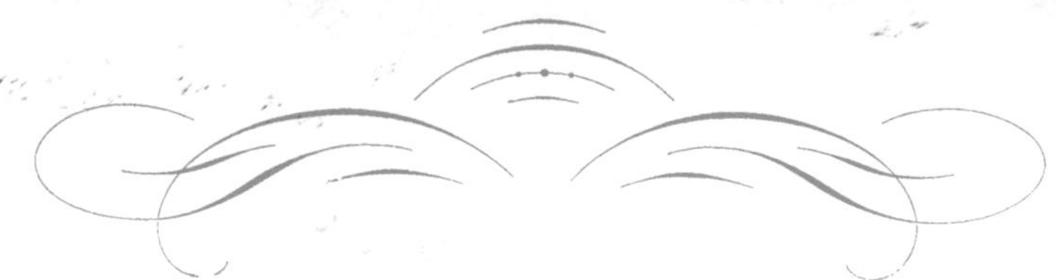

FRESH HERBAL TEAS

Fresh herbs are perfect for instant herbal tea, so it seems silly not to use them. I've always got a bunch of thyme knocking around in the fridge, as well as a thumb of ginger, and there'll usually be a bunch of rosemary, mint, or cilantro there, too. Those fancy herbal teas never get used quickly enough, leaving me with a cupboard full of out-of-date boxes. In my experience, there are very few people who drink herbal teas all the time, but lots of my friends do like to sip something light and herby late in the night after I've spent an evening stuffing them full of extraordinary food. I've now stopped buying special teas and I just use what's good and fresh.

My favorite way to serve herbal teas is to put mugs of hot water on the table alongside a few bundles of herbs, some slices of ginger and lemon, and some sugar, and let everyone make their own fragrant combinations. Fresh thyme is a winner, and rosemary is delicious, too, despite the fact that it has a reputation for bitterness when fresh. Bay leaf is good, parsley is wonderfully delicate, cinnamon and star anise are very interesting, and lightly spicy.

You have to drink the tea with the herbs still in it, but as long as they're on a sprig rather than in lots of little pieces, I prefer this to a soggy tea bag floating around. You can also buy empty tea bags ready to be filled with your own herbs and spices (see Suppliers, page 218). So instead of buying lots of expensive boxes of obscure flavor combinations, just open up your herb and spice cupboard and go to town.

MY SUGGESTIONS

- rosemary
- basil
- thyme
- mint
- ginger and lemon
- dill
- fresh rose petals
- lemongrass
- bay leaves
- cilantro
- parsley
- cinnamon
- a whole lime (the oils in the zest ooze out!)
- galangal (also called blue ginger)

Serve mugs of piping hot water with a selection of herbs and spices for your friends to help themselves, and put honey and sugar on the table, too.

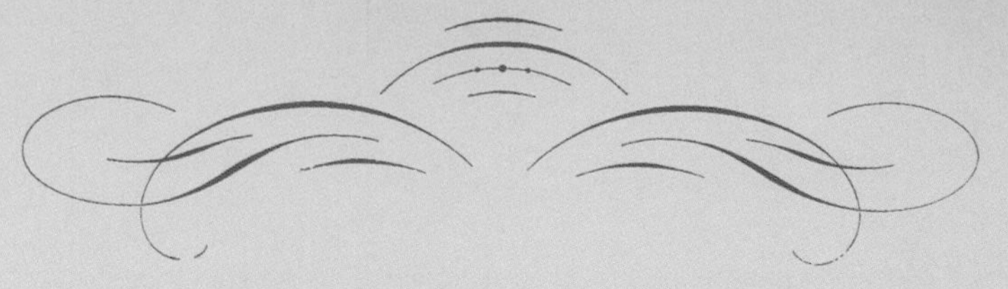

SLOE GIN

Sloes, or blackthorns, are little wild plums the size and color of a reddish-purpley grape. They're very astringent, so aren't much good for eating, but they do make an extraordinary deep-red, full-flavored drink when steeped in gin. Found in hedgerows across Britain, sloes are virtually unheard of in the United States. You'll likely have to use damson plums instead—they're rare, but can be found at farmers' markets. You'll also need a wide-necked bottle or a resealable jar, washed in boiling water.

1 ½ cups (half a bottle) gin
⅓ cup superfine sugar
½ teaspoon almond essence
9oz sloes (or damson plums), washed

Pour the gin, sugar, and almond essence into a sterilized bottle or jar and swill it around until the sugar has mostly dissolved. Prick the washed sloes all over with a needle—at least five pricks per sloe—then add them to the liquid and seal the bottle or jar tightly. Add a label and write the date on it. The sloes need to steep in the gin for at least 3 months. (Write the "ready" date on, too, to remind you.)

Store the bottle in a dark place and shake it every now and then—once a week, if you can remember. You can strain the sloe gin (through a piece of muslin or a clean dish towel) and rebottle it any time between 3 and 12 months after initial bottling. Serve as a neat liqueur.

LEMONADE

This lemonade tastes like you've squeezed pure sunshine into a glass and just added bubbles.

MAKES 2 QUARTS

1 ¼ cups sugar
6 lemons

TO SERVE
5 cups still or sparkling water
lots of ice

Put 1 cup water and the sugar in a pan and warm over low heat, stirring until the sugar has dissolved. Peel or grate the zest of one of the lemons, then juice all six lemons and stir zest and juice into the syrup. Pour into a bottle or pitcher and place in the fridge until fully chilled (about 30–60 minutes). To serve, mix with sparkling water and add ice.

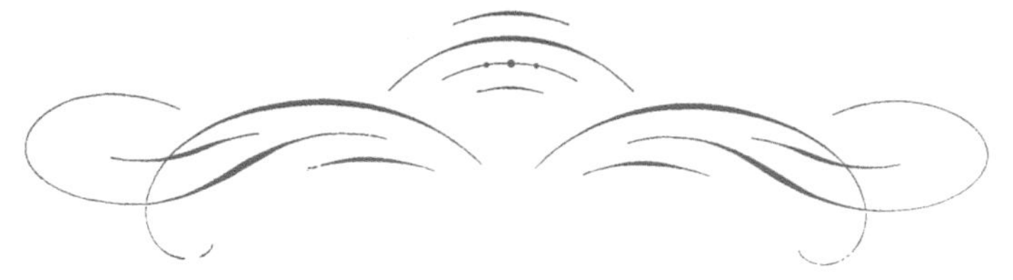

GINGER ALE

My mom always had a few bottles of ginger ale brewing, and every now and then one would blow up, with an impressive KaBOOOM. If you want to avoid explosions, it's simple: use plastic carbonated drinks bottles, which are made to cope with tremendous pressure.

This recipe takes only 20 minutes or so to make, but the ginger ale needs to be left to brew for a couple of days before it's ready to drink. You'll need 5 quarts' worth of bottles and a large saucepan that will hold 5 quarts of beer.

MAKES ABOUT 5 QUARTS

2 ½ cups superfine sugar
2 lemons, thickly sliced
2 tablespoons finely chopped fresh ginger
1 teaspoon cream of tartar
1 ½ teaspoons active dry yeast
(breadmaker's yeast is fine)

Measure 1 ½ quarts of water into a large saucepan and add the sugar, lemon slices, ginger, and cream of tartar. Bring to a boil, stirring the liquid to dissolve the sugar. Simmer for 5 minutes, then remove from the heat, and add another 3 quarts of cold water. Sprinkle in the yeast, stir it through, and put a lid on the pan. Place the pan in a cool place and leave it overnight.

In the morning, wash the bottles in very hot water. Strain the beer through a strainer to catch the ginger, then pour it into the bottles, leaving 2in of air at the top of each one. Screw the lids firmly onto the bottles and put them in a cool place to brew. It's this fermentation process that makes the beer fizzy and it will take 12–48 hours, depending on the temperature, for it to develop the right amount of fizz.

AN INSTANT VARIATION

If you feel you can't wait 2 days, try making this instant version. Mix together 1 thumb-sized piece of fresh ginger, peeled and grated, ⅓ cup unrefined sugar, and the zest and juice of 2 lemons. Leave to rest for 30 minutes, then strain and mix with sparkling water to taste. It's nice, but it's a different beast than the fermented version.

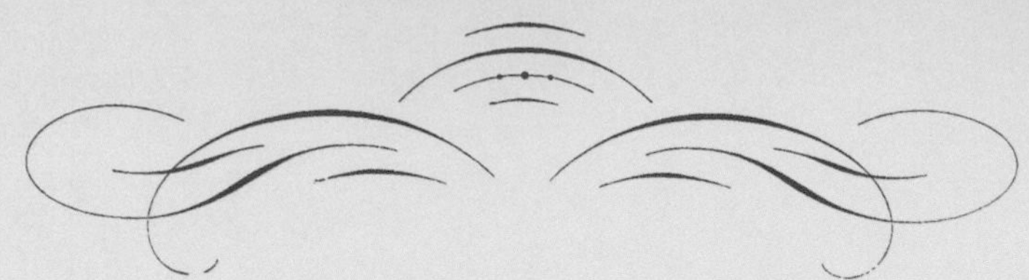

GATES-PEMBERTON MEGABRAND-SLAYING COLA

It's the ultimate secret recipe, jealously guarded by the world's largest drinks company, so there's a lovely little frisson of excitement when you create your own cola: Will you bust the megabrand? When you serve it to your friends, will the doors burst open and a SWAT team storm your kitchen and whisk you and your refreshing beverage off to an undisclosed location for interrogation? It would be a great story to tell—if they let you go before dessert.

Coca-Cola® began life in 1885 when the first version was invented as a medicine by a pharmacist named John Pemberton. It was initially an alcoholic drink called Pemberton's French Wine Cola, but was changed to nonalcoholic Coca-Cola® a year later. It was, by all accounts, quite a zippy little brew at first, made as it was from highly stimulating coca (from which cocaine is derived), caffeine-rich kola nuts, and an ingredient called damiana, which is purported to be both an aphrodisiac and, perhaps more plausibly, a cannabislike psychoactive drug.

I recently re-created Coke® on a TV show, which meant I was given the time of a lovely researcher named Natalie and a decent budget to buy lots of specialty ingredients to experiment with. I tried to perfect two recipes: a natural version using ingredients that are easy to find at your local supermarket, and a second one based on Pemberton's original recipe (or, at least, a recipe I found that claimed to be his original). My local pharmacy nearly called the cops when I asked if they could get their hands on any food-grade cocaine, and they nearly refused to sell me the caffeine tablets.

I tried all the different concoctions out on my girls, who both went a little bonkers after tasting the kola nuts (they'd never even drunk Coke®, bless 'em), but as taste-testers they were useless; they just preferred whichever drink contained the most sugar. I did a lot of tinkering, but finally I got pretty close to the original. Then I decided to go one step further and make some adjustments to the basic recipe to create something I thought tasted *better* than the original. When I hit on something that I really loved (a little more floral, slightly more sour, slightly less bitter, but slightly less sweet than modern Coke®), I took all my syrups along to the TV studio. We had a blind taste test with the TV show audience, and I am proud to say that I won by a landslide, with 85 percent claiming to prefer my brew.

The flavor base of cola is a combination of citrus fruit oils (from the zest), a few of the sweeter tasting spices, sourness from citrus fruit, and a bucketload of sweetness from refined and unrefined sugars. If you can lay your hands on some kola nuts, they add a great bitterness—and whizziness, too, since they are rich in caffeine! If you use the food-grade essential oils, you'll need to measure them using a set of micro-scales or a syringe bought from your local pharmacy.

Alright then—all I need for world domination is a multimillion-dollar marketing campaign, an integrated global distribution network, a bit of seed funding, and a bigger pan.

MAKES ENOUGH SYRUP FOR ABOUT 6 QUARTS OF COLA

FOR THE SYRUP
3¾ cups sugar
10 caffeine tablets (optional), ground to powder in a mortar and pestle (this will give about half the amount of caffeine found in a regular cola)
7 tablespoons freshly squeezed lime juice
3 tablespoons citric acid
1.5ml vanilla extract
2 tablespoons caramel
1oz kola nuts, finely crushed (optional)
grated zest of 2 lemons

FOR THE FLAVORING
1ml food-grade orange oil
0.5ml food-grade cinnamon oil
0.5ml food-grade nutmeg oil
0.5ml food-grade neroli oil
0.25ml food-grade coriander oil

TO SERVE
soda water

Pour 2 cups water into a pan and bring to a boil. Turn off the heat, then add the sugar, and stir until dissolved. Stir in all the remaining syrup ingredients and set aside.

Put all the flavored oils in a small blender (it has to be small, or the blades won't reach the level of the oils). Add 2 tablespoons of the syrup, or enough to cover the blades of the blender. Blend until the liquids have emulsified, then pour the contents of the blender into the remaining syrup (washing the blender out with a little extra syrup to get every last drop), and set aside to cool for 1 hour.

Strain the mixture through a piece of muslin or a clean dish towel into a pitcher, then transfer to a bottle. To serve, add soda water to the syrup at a ratio of 4:1; taste to see if it's to your satisfaction, adjusting the concentration, if needed.

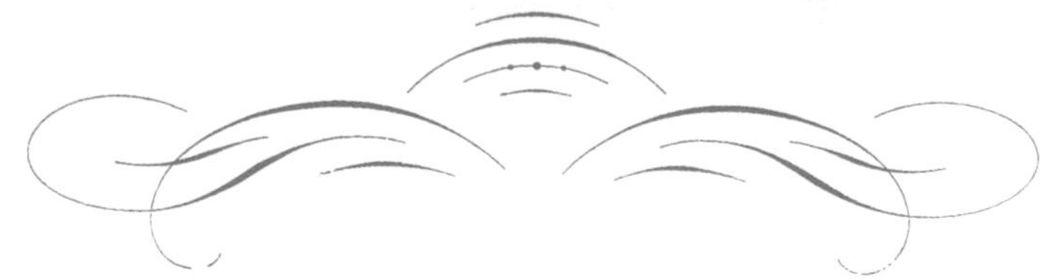

FOUR CLASSIC COCKTAILS

There really is nothing better to kick off a big night than a walloping good cocktail, especially if it's a martini. These outrageous concoctions are a beguiling mix of danger and sophistication combined with a gasping shock of sheer alcoholic power. Be careful, though. The great M. F. K. Fisher—an extraordinary woman who vies with Jean Anthelme Brillat-Savarin as my favorite, funniest, deadest food writer—once wrote that "One Martini is just right. Two Martinis are too many. Three Martinis are never enough." I've experimented with lots of different cocktails, but the reality is that I've never really needed any more than these four classics.

MARTINI

For sophistication and sheer power—careful, now. This is the classic, very dry version.

SERVES 1

2 shots (2oz) fine gin
¼ shot (¼oz) dry vermouth (i.e., Martini)
a handful of ice
a green olive or a long, thin strip of lemon peel, to serve

Pour the gin and vermouth into a cocktail shaker, add the ice, and shake to mix. Pour into a martini glass, add either an olive or a strip of lemon peel to garnish, and serve.

DANNY'S MARGARITA

If you're after a wild, whooping party atmosphere.

SERVES 1

2 shots (2oz) tequila
1 shot (1oz) Cointreau
1 shot (1oz) freshly squeezed lime juice
fine salt or popping candy (such as Pop Rocks) and a wedge of lime, to serve

Pour the tequila, Cointreau, and lime juice into a cocktail shaker and shake well to mix. Pour the salt or popping candy onto a small plate, wipe the rim of a martini glass with the lime slice to wet it a little, then dip it upside down on the plate to coat the rim (not too much—you don't want a mouthful of salt). Pour the cocktail into the glass and serve with the wedge of lime to suck on.

MOJITO

Dangerously easy-drinking, fun, and sweet. An ad man would probably say that this drink "skews young."

SERVES 1

2 teaspoons sugar
½ fresh lime, chopped into 4 pieces
10 fresh mint leaves
crushed ice (wrap ice cubes in a dish towel and beat with a rolling pin)
2 shots (2oz) rum
soda water, to taste

Put the sugar and lime chunks into a solid highball glass and muddle it (i.e., mash it up) with a pestle or soup spoon. Add the mint and muddle it some more. Fill the glass with crushed ice, then pour the rum in, and stir well. Add some soda water to the glass, stir again, and serve.

COSMOPOLITAN

This can be made conveniently in a pitcher and poured by the glass; multiply ingredients by the number of drinks.

SERVES 1

1 shot (1oz) vodka (preferably lemon flavored, but any will do)
1 shot (1oz) Cointreau or Grand Marnier
juice of ½ lime
2 shots (2oz) cranberry juice
ice, to serve

Pour all the ingredients except the ice into a cocktail shaker and shake to mix. Pour into a martini glass, add ice, and serve.

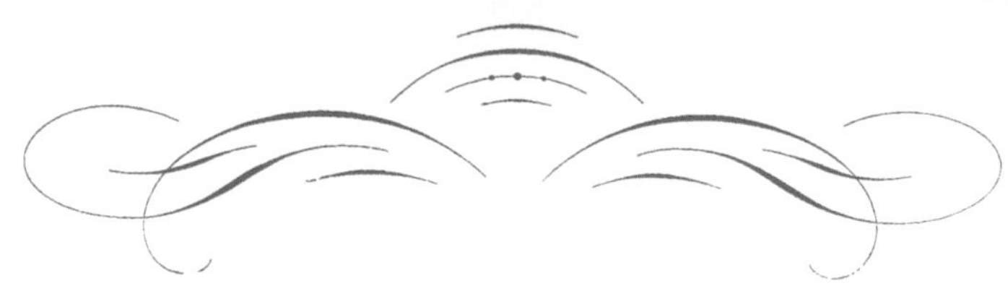

SUPPLIERS

Before you turn to the internet for your extraordinary supplies, take a look closer to home; you may be surprised at how many of the ingredients in this book are available (or can be ordered) from specialty and ethnic sources right on your doorstep, and I'd encourage you to buy them where a friendly face can give you advice or help you source what you need. I have my local favorites, and I know you'll find yours.

FROGS' LEGS
Available online from Cajun Grocer: www.cajungrocer.com
Linton's Seafood: www.lintonsseafood.com

RUSSIAN ROULETTE PADRÓN PEPPERS
Usually available fresh from well-stocked supermarkets and farmers' markets. Also available online from La Tienda: www.tienda.com

SEED SUPPLIERS
Burpee Seeds and Plants: www.burpee.com
Whatcom Seed Catalog online: www.seedrack.com

WEIRD AND WONDERFUL SNACKS
Asian Food Grocer: www.asianfoodgrocer.com
H Mart: www.hmart.com

INSECTS
Thailand Unique: www.thailandunique.com
Amazon: www.amazon.com

FOR THE LOVE OF JAMÓN
Whole Spanish hams and ham stands: Specializing in "the best of Spain," La Tienda sells whole high-end hams and stands online: www.tienda.com. For free shipping and a wealth of other gourmet Spanish goodies, try Raposos Gourmet and Tapas: www.raposogourmet.com

HAGGIS WITH WHISKEY, POTATOES, AND TURNIPS
Caledonian Kitchen: www.caledoniankitchen.com
McKean's: www.scottishhaggis.com

OSTRICH SCOTCH EGG
Available at upmarket supermarkets; some Whole Foods Markets stock them. Online from Exotic Meat Market: www.exoticmeatmarket.com

SUCKLING PIG
Try your local butcher first—he should be able to order one for you. If not, you can buy suckling pig online from D'Artagnan, the country's leading purveyor of organic game and poultry: www.dartagnan.com

… also Pig Roasts: pig roasting companies tend to be local, since they do their work on-site. Type "pig roast" into your search engine to find a company in your area.

APPLE CAVIAR
Sodium alginate, calcium chloride, micro-scales, and syringes are all available from Truffina™: www.truffina.com. The site even has a video demonstrating "caviar" making.

WHOLE BAKED VACHERIN CHEESE
Vacherin Mont d'Or, or similar variants, can be found at cheese shops and fine supermarkets. Buy online from Gourmet Food: www.gourmet-food.com

SHABU-SHABU, SUSHI & SASHIMI
Most major supermarkets stock the main Japanese ingredients such as sushi rice, nori seaweed, rice vinegar, soy and shoyu sauces. Ponzu (a lemony soy sauce), sesame dipping sauce, and rolling mats are often available as well, or can be bought from local Asian supermarkets.
For online shopping try:
Asian Food Grocer: www.asianfoodgrocer.com
H Mart: www.hmart.com
Amazon: www.amazon.com

COOKIE-TIN SMOKED SALMON
Hardwood or fruitwood chips are often available from the big supermarkets around summer (i.e., barbecuing) time, but are also available from some garden centers and online from Charcoal Store: www.charcoalstore.com

GOLDEN CHICKEN
Edible gold and silver transfer leaf (buy 23ct or over):
Amazon: www.amazon.com

FLUORESCENT JELLO
UV "blacklight" lamps can be bought from Blacklight: www.blacklight.com

POP-ROCKS-ENCRUSTED PINEAPPLE CARPACCIO
Pop Rocks Candy: www.poprockscandy.com
Old Time Candy: www.oldtimecandy.com

FRESH HERB TEAS
Empty, fillable tea bags can be bought from Amazon: www.amazon.com

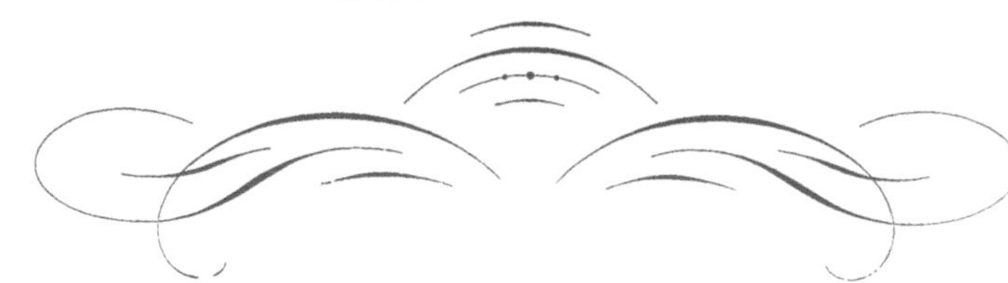

INDEX

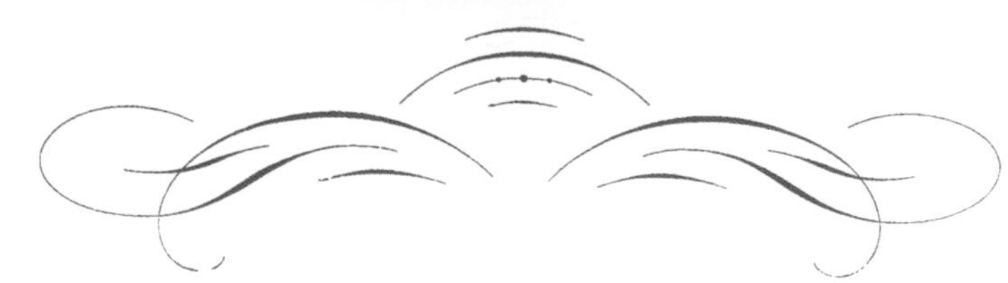

D

E

F

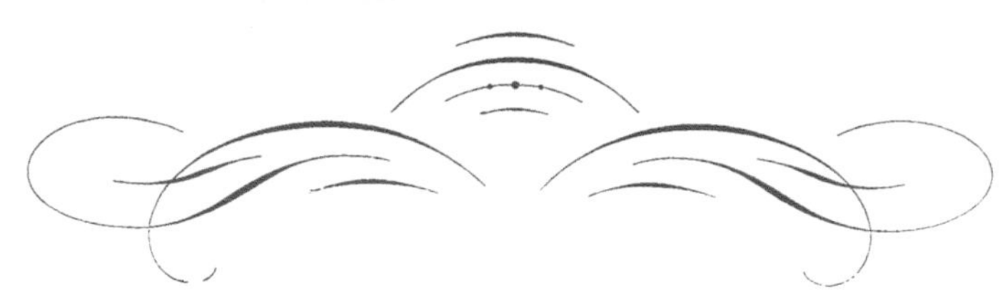

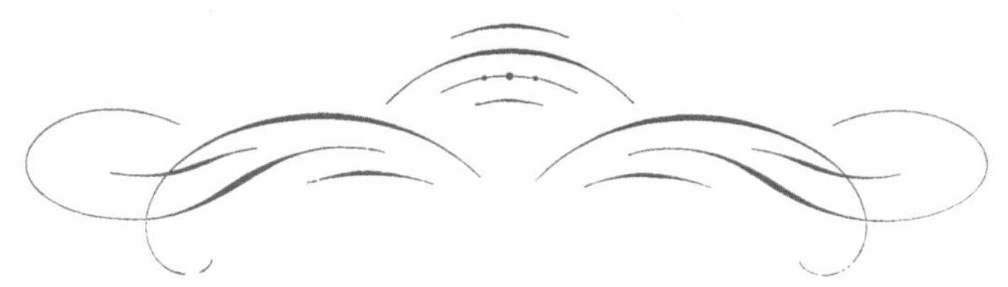

T

U

V

W

Z

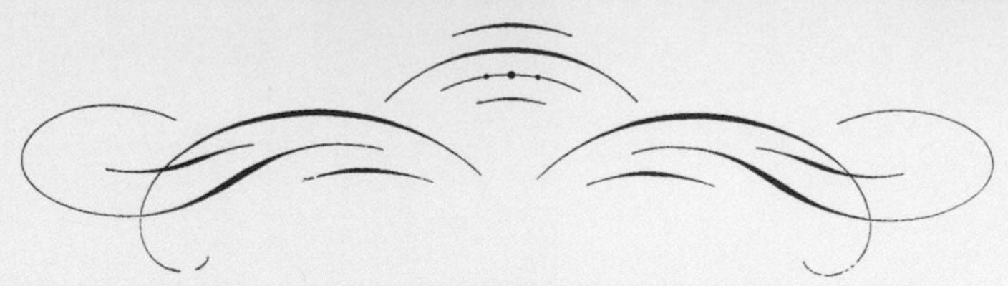

ACKNOWLEDGMENTS

I've wanted to own this book ever since I started to cook, so I'm fantastically proud and very grateful that Kyle Cathie let me write it. Praise be to Georgia for breathing extraordinary life into it (it really is beyond the call of duty to work with your main squeeze) and to Daisy and Poppy—not just for being in so many of her photos, but also for encouraging me to play with my food and for trying out so many of my hare-brained ideas. The only way that those ideas have taken book form is through the excitement, expertise, and creativity of Jenny Wheatley, Marina Filippelli, Lindsay Milne Mcleod, Judith Hannam, Sue Prescott, and Georgie Clarke, Two Associates, Laura Fyfe, Eve Teixeira, and Amanda Booth.

I've genuinely spent years looking for the *Extraordinary Cookbook*, but it turned out that it didn't exist except in fragments in my fevered mind and scattered among the writings of a thousand brilliant writers, from Jean Anthelme Brillat-Savarin to Heston Blumenthal, from Calvin H. Schwabe to Hugh Fearnley-Whittingstall. So I'd like to say thank you to all the authors of the books, magazines, newspapers, and TV and radio programs whose ideas have inspired all this. I hope I haven't lifted anything wholesale!

Thanks to Jonathan Glynn-Smith for taking the suckling pig and author photos and to Fiona and Zoe Cox for letting us shoot crayfish, toffee apples, and pumpkins at their beautiful house. Thanks to everyone who lent a little bit of their souls by appearing in the photos, especially Isaac and June, Alex (Zoe), Orlando (Hoops), Marni, Gabriel, Toby Farrant, Catharine, Eddie and Mark, Dora, Jo and Pia Glynn-Smith.

The following people helped to make this book either directly or indirectly, whether they were aware of it or not: Borra Garson, Jan Croxon, Emma Hughes, Paul Gilheaney, and all of the Gastronuts team at Objective and at the BBC, as well as all the wonderful kids who came on the show, the *Market Kitchen* team (especially the researchers), Andrea Sella, Will Daws, Kari Lia, Jack Storm, Karen O'Connor, Janice Hadlow, Gary Hunter, Bompass & Parr, Michelle Kass, Dora Hegyi, Nick Gibson, Chris Godfrey, Jean Gates, Nicky Ross, Harriet and Mark, Eric Gates, Anneka, Angus and Barney for the secret oyster hunt, Tom Gates, Thomas Cara, Jean-Anthelme, and all my friends who've joined in these extraordinary feasts.